W9-BZG-550

OUTNUMBERED!

RAISING 13 KIDS WITH HUMOR AND PRAYER

Mary Ann Kuharski

SERVANT
BOOKS

PUBLISHED BY ST. ANTHONY MESSENGER PRESS
CINCINNATI, OHIO

Scripture passages have been taken from *New Revised Standard Version Bible*, copyright ©1989 by the Division of Christian Education of the National Council of the Churches of Christ in the U.S.A., and used by permission. All rights reserved.

Cover design by Mark Sullivan
Cover illustration by Dave Hile
Book design by Phillips Robinette, O.F.M.

LIBRARY OF CONGRESS CATALOGING-IN-PUBLICATION DATA

Kuharski, Mary Ann.
  Outnumbered! : raising 13 kids with humor and prayer / Mary Ann Kuharski.
     p. cm.
  ISBN 0-86716-734-3 (pbk. : alk. paper) 1. Kuharski, Mary Ann. 2. Catholics—Biography. 3. Family—Religious life. 4. Family—Anecdotes. 5. Parenting—Religious aspects—Catholic Church. 6. Child rearing—Religious aspects—Catholic Church. 7. Parent and child—Religious aspects—Catholic Church. I. Title.

BX4705.K75845A3 2006
282.092—dc22

2005024631

ISBN-13: 978-0-86716-734-4
ISBN-10: 0-86716-734-3

Copyright ©2006 Mary Ann Kuharski. All rights reserved.

Published by Servant Books, an imprint of St. Anthony Messenger Press.
28 W. Liberty St.
Cincinnati, OH 45202
www.AmericanCatholic.org

Printed in the United States of America.

Printed on acid-free paper.

06 07 08 09 10 5 4 3 2 1

CONTENTS

Introduction vii

1 Parenting: A *New* Dimension 1

2 Kids' Décor 5

3 What's in a Name? 9

4 Too Many Kids? 13

5 Words of Life 18

6 The Gift of Love 23

7 Unsung Heroines 28

8 What's It Like in a BIG Family? 32

9 Favorite Memories of Mom 38

10 Taking Toddlers to Church 42

11 Married to the Coupon King 47

12 The Family That Plays Together,
Stays Together 52

13 Boys and Their Toys 56

14 The Rules Are the Rules! 60

15 Mom's Remedy for Naughty Talk 65

16 Dealing With the Unexpected 69

17 Excuses, Excuses! 73

18 A Retreat for the Teens in Your Life 76

19 Weight Lifting Your Way to Heaven? 80

20 Gen and Lu 84

21 Do I Get a Trophy? 89

22 Parents Can Come in Handy 93

23 What About Manners and Modesty? 97

24 Wedding Plans 102

25 How Many Priests Can We Fit at the
Dinner Table? 107

26 Christmas Memories 113

27 Children: Blessings, Not Burdens! 117

28 The Engagement Blessing 121

29 "Thanks, Mr. President!" 126

30 God's Children by Adoption 130

31 A Father's View 134

32 The Adventure Begins 145

33 Tina and Tony Fly In 150

34 Responding to God's Nudging 157

35 Learning to Trust 168

36 Blessings and Humblings 178

37 Our Last Hurrah! 187

38 Open Letter to a Child 191

Notes 196

To my husband, John, who contributed more than just a chapter. He is my sounding board, best friend and partner in this "love story" of *Outnumbered! Raising 13 Kids With Humor and Prayer.*

To the Blessed Mother Mary and to Saint Joseph, who never fail to hear my prayers—always bringing me closer to their Son.

And to all of you who strive to be faithful parents as God calls you to be. Let us never be sidetracked, always remembering that our number one goal is heaven—for our children and ourselves! After all, these children who are placed in our care, whether by "tummy" or adoption, are merely on loan from a heavenly Father who loves us and wants us with him forever.

Introduction

I am certainly no authority on family life and never intended to be a writer. On the contrary, I was busy, and more than content, in my role as a full-time homemaker and mother. But it came to the point where I could no longer ignore the influence of a radical feminist movement and dominant secular media, which routinely seemed to denigrate motherhood, marriage and children. I began to feel as if they were referring to second-class citizens when children and motherhood were the focus.

The message to at-home mothers, sometimes subtle and sometimes shrill, was direct and deliberate: "Smart women choose meaningful, fulfilling careers *outside* the home. Only the not-so-bright or the well-to-do would choose homemaking and motherhood full-time."

They were not speaking for me! I wanted to rent a plane and write across the sky, "Listen, Sweethearts, there is no paycheck, no title, no fringe benefits, retirement plan or lottery win that could ever pay me enough to wipe these noses and bottoms. I do it for free and for the love of God, and there are millions of moms in America today just like me!"

There are millions of mothers like me, who are in the home, loving their husbands, caring for their children and seeing God as the grace-giver to help in their vocational call. That's right: motherhood is a *vocational call*, not a job, a career or a "part-time" role. We are building up God's mystical body. Once a mother, always a mother!

We need to encourage and energize each other in our vocation, especially in this anti-child, anti-family culture. And thus the reason for my first book, *Raising Catholic Children* (Our Sunday Visitor Press), which tells of the Kuharski journey in faith as we became parents to thirteen children: seven by "tummy," as our children say, and six by "airport" or adoption. In this first writing our children were tots to teens, and the issues reflected the daily dimensions of our lives at that time.

A few years later, at the prompting of young Catholic parents, I published my second book, *Parenting with Prayer* (Our Sunday Visitor Press). Here I attempted to respond to the question of many young parents, "How do we teach our children about our faith?" *Parenting with Prayer* covered issues of faith from this mom's everyday perspective: the sacraments; corporal and spiritual works of mercy; heaven, hell and purgatory (yes, there is such a place!).

One section dealt with helping our children understand the importance of making a good confession. (I had one adolescent son who said he didn't commit any sin and did not have to go. I offered to write him a list and pack him a lunch!) The book also included sections on the rosary and daily prayer.

Three years later came *Building a Legacy of Love* (Queenship Publishing). I wrote this in response to Christian parents who were seeking support in dealing with issues of puberty, adolescence, discipline, teen demands and outside influences.

Outnumbered! Raising 13 Kids with Humor and Prayer is written for Catholic parents and people of all faiths, be they first-time parents needing a few tips on parenting (see "Taking Toddlers to Church," "What About Manners and Modesty?" "The Rules Are the Rules!" "What's It Like in a

BIG Family?") or more "seasoned" parents who are look-ing for a faith-based relationship with their teens and young adults.

Many who read my monthly columns (in *The Catholic Servant* and *Lay Witness* magazine) or previous books have asked, "Where are your children, and what are they doing today?" Chapters 32 through 37 answer these questions, giving some specifics about the kids you have come to know through my earlier writings.

This book offers an honest and candid portrayal of the blessings as well as the bumps and bruises that John and I have encountered in our *vocational call* to raise our large and diverse family. I hope to encourage and inspire you in your own effort to live out your vocational call, whatever it may be, as we all continue to strive for the ulti-mate prize: heaven!

> What no eye has seen, nor ear heard,
>   nor the human heart conceived,
> what God has prepared for those who love him.
> —1 CORINTHIANS 2:9

1

Parenting: A *New* Dimension

I still remember the panic I felt during my first pregnancy at the prospect of becoming a mother. Motherhood seemed pretty elementary, from what I'd observed, yet the thought of one so little being totally dependent on ME was another story indeed. Was I ready? Not really. My husband, John, seemed more sure of himself.

I decided to check out a bundle of books on the subject from the library. Surely there were authorities on parenting who could give me a crash course on the "dos and don'ts" for my new role of mothering. When I got to the "expert" who advocated "shared decision making" and allowing children the "freedom" to choose their own religion, I returned the books and decided to count on God's grace and our own common sense.

Thankfully, John and I were surrounded by loving family and friends. They saw us through the "new parent" jitters—even those first months with a colicky little one.

Children, we learned, are nothing short of amazing. They have an uncanny way of turning our plans, our dreams, our world upside down and getting us to like it! Of course, we were in love.

Yes, life takes on a whole new dimension once a child enters your heart and home. Whether you have one on your hip or ten at your table, life is *never* quite the same.

Take sleep, for instance. We had been pretty much in control of when we went to bed and when we awoke. And on most days we awoke rested and refreshed from an uninterrupted eight-hour night. No more! Back when our first little imp didn't reach our kneecaps, she wielded more power over our lives than the president of the United States. Our nights became totally dependent on her good nature.

As we outgrew the midnight feedings, the toddler, adolescent and beyond years offered their own shares of anxious evenings. We lived through the occasional nightmares, influenza and other childhood diseases, first-time drivers with the family car and the ultimate worry: courtship and dating.

Does a parent *ever* get eight hours of sleep? Why would I tell and spoil all the fun?

Another major adjustment dealt with our time alone. Finding an evening to go out together could be a major challenge. Sometimes it seemed as if the mere mention of a date night brought on an epidemic of twenty-four-hour flu or a mysterious rash.

But manage we did, and on those occasions when we were stuck at home, we knew we were in it together. Let's face it: No family has ever really bonded until they have experienced a case of poison ivy, chicken pox (with a two-week incubation time) or, worst of all, head lice!

Then there's the issue of privacy. Children are like sponges. They seem to absorb our moods, manners and messages, only to imitate them later. Never assume they're not listening. I learned my lesson the year one of our kids announced during "current events" in a social studies class, "My mom is expecting, but she's not ready to tell everyone yet!"

Kids will affect your physical appearance, too. Bring a baby home to stay, and it's not long before your sleek and chic look—where everything matches and looks fairly crisp, clean and fresh—bears telltale signs of spills and spit-ups and exudes undefined aromas.

You'll also begin to sport new "accessories." Cute little handbags give way to diaper bags, "carryalls" and children's backpacks. Forget those pretty little scarves tied casually around the neck and shoulders; you'll want a burp cloth there, hopefully clean, to protect what remains of your wardrobe.

As for jewelry, I had a total of three sets of earrings— one gold, one silver, one pearl (fake, of course). This cut down on the problem of trying to find a pair that matched. My stash of unused pins and unmatched earrings eventually became Barbie doll accessories or parts of the kids' "dress-up" collection.

It didn't take me long to discover that there was little time to be stylish or "in." I became more focused on just *getting there* and having everything I *needed* when I arrived. There's nothing worse than having to leave an event early because the baby messed the *only* change of clothes you brought—a harsh lesson I learned and occasionally relearned.

Worse was when the baby managed to mess *my* outfit as well. This is when a mother becomes downright resourceful. Your choices are (1) leave for home NOW, (2) see if you can borrow something to wear from the hostess or (3) keep your coat on—no matter what the room temperature is. I've done all three!

So some may wonder, why in the world would seem-ingly intelligent adult men and women forsake the entice-ment of a carefree, childless life, with its promise of restful nights, peaceful days, orderly homes (see the next chapter) and perhaps luxuries besides, to be called Mommy and Daddy? The answer is simple: LOVE.

There is no home, no job, no pet, no luxury that can compare to the love of a child. Who but a child can change our minds, rearrange our lives, steal our hearts and con-vince us to pray for more? 🌲

> For where your treasure is, there will your heart be also.
>
> —MATTHEW 6:21

2

Kids' Décor

Unless the LORD builds the house, those who build it labor in vain.

—PSALM 127:1

Once kids entered the scene, our home also took on a new look. For nearly twenty years we bypassed the urge to do rooms in soft creams, whites and yellows—colors I yearned to see—and chose instead browns, greens and golds, which had the distinct advantage of blending in with grass stains and dirt!

When the walls occasionally manifested free-form crayon or Magic Marker drawings (trust me: there's nothing *magic* about them), we discovered the value of quick-drying latex paint. I'll bet money whoever invented this paint had a few little smudges of his own to remove!

Our furniture and accessories began to have that *distressed* or "lived-in" appearance, complete with "love prints." We chuckled when we saw furniture advertised as *new* that looked as if it had been chain-whipped by a motorcycle gang. "Just think," I told John, "some people go to great lengths to find even one piece of furniture that looks like that, and then they spend lots of money for it. And we have a whole houseful!"

As to collectibles and such, K.I.S.S. ("Keep It Simple, Stupid") became my motto when our kids were small. We had few knickknacks, by choice. Why make my job more stressful by having a home that was not "child friendly"?

John and I were more interested in making sure our children felt our love and encouragement than in fretting over smudge marks or worrying about a collection of things that would *never* be able to hug and love the way a little child can.

Now, maybe you enjoy anxiety, are a glutton for punishment or are doing at-home testing for a market research firm on the number of minutes it takes a child to destroy a precious collectible. If not, I'd say your days of crystal, blown glass, Hummel figurines and imported artwork are limited once a little one enters the scene. Installing high shelves might help; postponing your hobby is somewhat more realistic.

Don't get me wrong. I enjoy looking at art as much as the next person. I even admit to an occasional lapse in judgment, when I bring something home that "I just couldn't resist." It doesn't take long, however, before someone hears me say, "Well, I guess it just proves I can't have anything that isn't chipped or broken around here."

I gave up on smelly sachets after I discovered the remains of a packet of peach blossoms scattered across the bathroom floor. Take it from me, the vacuum that can pick up all those little petals and pieces has *not* been invented. Worse yet was finding the miniature flakes attached to every piece of black clothing I had placed in the dryer. Yup, one of my little friends had tossed a sachet in the dryer "to make all the clothes smell good."

It only took one experience of scrubbing wax off piano keys and air vents to realize that scented candles would not be part of the Kuharski décor. And a tub running over with bubbles sent those beautiful bubble bath crystals out the door.

But you can't forgo a Christmas tree! Our problems

here diminished after we began wiring our tree to the wall and ceiling. We learned this lesson the year one of our sons managed to pull the tree over three times in a week.

Even the yard takes on a new image with children. Let's be honest: Weedless turf and manicured gardens are for the retiree. Parents may begin to notice that their grass appears in blotches—scattered among the sandbox, the swing set, the tree house and those enticing mudholes.

On the plus side, there's no need for "edging" when you have kids, as nearly every edge has been worn away by tire treads and tennis shoes. Bikes, trikes, wagons, scooters, skateboards, three-wheeled pushcarts, hoops and hockey nets dominate areas once reserved for cars, walkways and grass.

"Is someone having a garage sale?" a prospective neighbor once asked in surveying the bikes and paraphernalia in our backyard and driveway.

"Oh, no, it's just our kids and a few of their friends," I responded politely.

There was an unmistakable look of panic on the woman's face as she hurried to her car with the realtor in hasty pursuit. Needless to say, she did *not* move into the neighborhood.

Yes, we taught our children cleanliness, manners and respect for property. But children are children, not robots, kewpie dolls or adults who can control their every move. (Neither can we, the last time I noticed!)

Now that there are no little ones in the home, and our three remaining here—with their schooling and schedules—seem to have more of a life than we do, we have a newfound interest in gardening and decorating our home. "Believe me, our house didn't look like this when I lived here," our son Tim once told his bride-to-be. He was right.

But that was when *he* and his brothers and sisters were the focal point of our every day.

What we wore, what we drove (station wagons and vans) and how we decorated our home revolved around them. Our measure was, "Does it blend well with children?" If it didn't, it could wait. This was a loving rule to live by, and one we will never regret. 🌳

3

What's in a Name?

By faith our ancestors received approval.
—HEBREWS 11:2

"**W**hy do we name babies after the saints or some of those 'old people' from the Bible?" my son Joseph (then nine) asked at dinner one evening. Joseph's older brother Tim and his wife, Tina, had announced that they were expecting their first baby. Recalling that all of our children were given what I describe as "strong saints names," we talked about the tradition of naming a child after a saint of old.

"At baptism every person becomes a member of God's family. When parents give an infant the name of a saint, they are calling on that special saint to watch over, pray for and protect that baby. The saint then becomes that child's patron saint," I explained.

"So that's what that means!" Joseph responded. "You mean like Saint Charles is praying for Charlie, Saint Anthony for Tony, Saint Dominic for Dominic, Saint Michael for Michael and Saint Joseph for me?"

"That's it! And let me tell you, they have their work cut out for them," I added.

The *Catechism of the Catholic Church* says:

In baptism, the Lord's name sanctifies man, and the Christian receives his name in the Church. This can be the name of a saint, that is, of a disciple who has lived a life of exemplary fidelity to the Lord. The

> patron saint provides a model of charity; we are
> assured of his intercession. The 'baptismal name' can
> also express a Christian mystery or Christian virtue.
> 'Parents, sponsors, and the pastor are to see that a
> name is not given which is foreign to Christian senti-
> ment.'" (*CCC*, #2156, quoting canon 855)

Most parents are downright picky about their children's names, sometimes taking months to narrow the choices. And rightly so. A name is a very personal thing; it will identify that child all through life.

Sometimes a name's special meaning is significant for a parent. Just look at the wall plaques and baby name books on the market. Often the name of a parent, grandparent, favorite relative or friend is chosen, because that person is someone the child can look up to, even if only in memory. We Christians choose a name because of the patron's good and faithful life.

Sadly, there are those today who do not know or deliberately reject such customs, favoring instead a more "progressive" image for their young. And so we meet children with cute and catchy titles, perhaps those of celebrities or cities or something flowery and fun.

I couldn't help but wince when a new mother who shared my hospital room after a delivery named her baby after a new perfume fragrance. No, it wasn't Obsession. I held my tongue, but my thought was, "You mean there are *no* relatives or friends, no saints or biblical heroes this child can identify with or look up to? It's got to be a bottle of perfume?"

There was no debate at our house about what type of names we would choose for our children. Assigning a patron saint to a child at baptism seemed to us the best spiritual "jump start" we could offer. We wanted all thirteen to have a saint or angel on their side. We wanted them, from the very beginning of their lives, to have all the prayers and protection we could muster.

We also wanted them to identify early on with winners! And what greater winner can there be than one who has "fought the good fight," "finished the race" and "kept the faith," as Saint Paul wrote (2 Timothy 4:7)? After all, isn't the ultimate goal of every Christian parent to *guide their young to heaven?*

Father Mark Dosh, pastor of St. John the Baptist Church of Excelsior, Minnesota, offered this explanation about the Catholic tradition of naming children after the saints: "It sets us in the *larger family of the church.* Just as little brothers and sisters look up to their older brothers and sisters, we are reminded of Saint Francis of Assisi, Saint Paul of Tarsus, Saint Teresa of Avila and all the other heroes of the church. We recall their heroic efforts on behalf of the faith. When we examine their lives more closely, we also see their faults and how they overcame them through faith. This offers us hope in our own walk in faith."

The communion of saints is rooted in the one life of Christ. We are *all* taken into his family at baptism. Saint Peter with his denial, Saint Thomas with his doubts, Saint Paul with his persecution of Christians and Saint Augustine with his early life of debauchery are but a few of the heroes who relied on God's forgiveness and grace, overcame their past and became great saints of the church.

"In a very real sense," Father continued, "we are members of the same family through baptism. The saints are our older brothers and sisters, people we take pride in knowing about and trying to emulate. They overcame their own struggles to achieve great accomplishments, to live the faith and to hand it down for generations."

Speaking of baptism, Saint Maximilian Kolbe once wrote, "The soul is reborn by water in Baptism and so becomes a child of God.... Child of God, member of the family of God, God the Father is your Father, the Mother of God is your mother, the Son of God is your Brother. You become a co-heir of God, bound by and in love with the Persons of that Divine Family."[1]

How blessed we are to be members of this communion of saints, with such a rich and powerful heritage of faith, handed down through generations to us. Now we in turn can offer it to our own young. 🌳

> The good leave an inheritance to their children's children.
>
> —PROVERBS 13:22

4

Too Many Kids?

Pope John Paul II said, "Motherhood is an incessant message in favor of human life, since it speaks, even without words, against everything that destroys it and threatens it. It is impossible to find anything that is in greater opposition to war and slaughter than motherhood."[1]

I recently met a woman who introduced me to her first child. She just glowed as she looked down at the infant she cradled in her arms. "We waited twenty years for her," she told me. "I don't know why, but we never felt led to adopt during that time. We just waited. We knew God had a plan."

And so he did. Her faith and witness reminded me of the Blessed Mother's cousin Elizabeth, who was older than most when she became pregnant with John the Baptist. "Elizabeth in her old age has also conceived a son; and this is the sixth month for her who was said to be barren. For nothing will be impossible with God" (Luke 1:36–37).

Most of us know couples who would eagerly welcome a child in their lives. Some try for years to have children, without success. Those of us with children may never understand the emotional roller coaster they ride as they hope, pray and wait for what is not to be. God reads their hearts and will surely bless their faithfulness and openness to his will. Some feel led to adopt; others do not. *All* are deserving of our prayers and support.

What a contrast these couples are to those who refuse to be open to the possibility of God's gift of new life in their marriage. They reject outright God's plan and allow no room for a child in their lives.

Up until a few decades ago children were considered "gifts from God." In fact, most faiths included children as a "blessing" and welcomed them in the wedding ceremony. Today many faiths consider such a mention "politically incorrect," even *offensive* or intrusive.

Imagine: children as *offensive!*

Indeed, organizations such as Planned Parenthood and Zero Population Growth have had a chilling effect on America's attitude toward what was once considered our greatest natural resource. There are organized groups committed to "nonparenting," such as No Kidding. More militant groups, such as Negative Population Growth, advocate tax incentives to punish those who would have more than two children. It's no coincidence that well over one million unborn babies are killed legally each year in our country.

A mindset against children—or at least "too many children"—has permeated even some traditional Christian thinking. Just ask any young couple expecting even their third child how many times they have heard, "Was this *planned?*" (It was—by God!) Or, "Weren't you using something?" (As if they were *supposed* to.) Or, "Not again? Is this it for you?" Or, "Don't you know about overpopulation?" (My next chapter offers some loving but firm responses to these types of questions.)

Most disappointing of all for expecting couples is being targeted by family and friends. You would hope these people would offer encouragement and support!

Expecting parents sometimes need an emotional shield to protect them from the verbal blows of those who not so gently insinuate, "You should not be having another child." Our prayers, support and even a gentle hug can be that shield of love for them.

Clearly, not everyone is meant to parent a large family. There are couples who cannot have children. Other people never get married, for that matter. Some are needed by loved ones who are sick or shut in, with demands that may drain their time and attention far more than a household of children. Others may be called to serve as vital role models and mentors to young children in their extended family, community or work.

God has a perfect and unique plan for each of us: married, single or religious, large family or small. The key is to be "open" to his way.

There was a time in my youth when my goals were little more than a career and a convertible. Thank heavens, God didn't take me seriously. When I met my Polish Prince, God began to reshape my thinking. Out went the car, out went the career and out went my selfish, narrow vision, as prayer and a relinquishment to his will brought something far more precious than I could have dreamed.

Did we envision having thirteen children, six coming by adoption with special needs? Not on your life! Isn't God good? He doesn't spring things on us all at once but lets us get used to an idea one step at a time. Think what we would have missed had we not been open!

What can we do to stand up for life in our culture?

- Be aware of how words hurt, especially for those who are childless and yearn for family, as well as for those who are enlarging their families. A hug and a prayer should be our loving response in both situations.

- Beware of anti-child culture and rhetoric. There should be no room in our vocabulary for phrases such as "unwanted children." All are gifts from God—including the "surprises" to us. All are part of his *perfect* design, and God has a *mission* for each to fulfill. Thus we have another reason why abortion is so horrible: It destroys the part of God's plan that that child was created to fulfill.

- Don't be fooled by those who claim that there is an overpopulation problem. Hunger in particular areas of the world may be a problem of distribution or a result of war, a catastrophic natural disaster or a totalitarian dictator. No matter the problem, our response should *never* be to eliminate God's children.

- Over sixty-nine countries, including all of Europe, have populations that are below replacement level, falling off as their citizenry advances in age. France offers a subsidy and one year's rent to those who will have a child; Japan has resorted to a five thousand dollar incentive. In Italy a mayor of one town is urging a tax on those who are childless.[2]

- If you are expecting a child, begin each day with a prayer to the Blessed Mother and one to Saint Gerard, the patron saint of expectant mothers. Both of them will pray for your health and strength.

✐ And if you are longing for a child, pray, "Good Saint Gerard, powerful intercessor before the throne of God, wonder worker of our day, I call upon you and seek your aid. You know that our marriage has not as yet been blessed with a child, and you know how much we desire this gift. Please present our fervent pleas to the Creator of life, from whom all parent-hood proceeds, and beseech him to bless us with a child whom we may raise as a child and heir of heaven. Amen."

✐ Love the children God has put in your life—be they sons or daughters, neighbors or friends—and thank him for them every day. 🌳

5

Words of Life

Y ou have *how* many kids?" is the usual response we get
from those who hear we have thirteen.

As "inconceivable" as it may seem, we can't imagine
our lives any other way. While I will readily concede that
parenting a large family is not for everyone, for John and
me it was like the old potato chip commercial. We couldn't
stop after one!

Of course there were times we hesitated and ques-
tioned our sanity, and maybe each other as well, but all in
all, each time we "broadened our horizons"—and, yes,
there were some "surprises" along the way—we saw the
power of God's love in our lives.

You might say we cheated a bit, because only seven of
our children came by "tummy" and the other six by "airport," as the kids would say. Two came from orphanages in
Vietnam, one from the Philippines and one from Calcutta,
India. One is Mexican American, and one is a biracial
American. All the adopted children had special needs. In
truth we may have started out thinking *we* were going to
do something for them, but in reality it was *they* who did
far more for us. Their mere presence reminded us daily of
the *real* meaning and purpose of life!

All in all, parenting a large family worked for us
because we were unified in our purpose—even when we

weren't sure we knew what we were doing! God was at the helm. "I led them with cords of human kindness, with bands of love. I was to them like those who lift infants to their cheeks [or 'who ease the yoke on their jaws']" (Hosea 11:4).

Yet we, like most parents, never made it through a pregnancy—or an adoption for that matter—without a barrage of well-meaning and not-so-well meaning inquiries. It seemed the moment I began to "show" the questions surfaced. In some people's minds it was "generous" of us to adopt but "selfish" of us to conceive. Of course, issues of race, age and handicap fueled some challenging comments when we were set to adopt, but the most prying and critical words were reserved for what was viewed as our "lack of planning."

What is it about the sight of a pregnant woman or expecting couple that can unleash the best and the worst in people?

The *best* are those who extend congratulations, a hug or even a little something for the new baby or the family. I sincerely believe that God has a special place in heaven for those who rush over with hot dishes and baked goods after a new baby's arrival.

On the other hand, there are those who treat the news of a new baby as if they'd just learned the mother had been diagnosed with an incurable illness or had volunteered for kamikaze pilot training. John and I have heard everything from "Was this planned?" to "Don't tell me you're pregnant again!" to "Your husband needs a night job." A few of John's least favorites were *"Reeeeally?* How did *that* happen?" "Weren't you using anything?" "Haven't you ever heard of the PILL?"

Through the years we learned to take an insensitive remark in stride, "offer it up" (as a prayer for the offender) and sometimes lighten it with a laugh. After about the fifth child there actually seemed to be less sarcasm and criticism. Perhaps people thought we were past the point of education, help or shame. Thank heavens!

In the meantime, here are some of the responses we offered—or wished we had the courage to offer—to those who were less than enthusiastic about our "new baby" joy.

When someone said, "I'm sure glad it's *YOU* and not me!" I'd say, "So am I! We're thrilled!"

Or, "You're NOT pregnant *again?*" "Yes. Aren't we lucky?"

"What about your *age* (health, job, other children, your mother's neighbor or whatever)?" "Well, God must think we can handle it."

"But you're so *young* (so old, so busy, so tired, so lazy, so sick, so in shape, so out-of-shape and so on)." "We're trying for the *Guinness Book of World Records!*"

"Was this planned? Were you using anything?" "No. Were we supposed to?" (They never quite know what to do with that). We want to remind them kindly that *all* babies are planned and wanted by God. And God makes *no* mistakes.

"Are you sure you know what you're doing?" We wouldn't respond to this one, just smile. Of course we don't know what we're doing, but God does!

"How nice, but how can you *afford another* one?" (They don't really think it's all that nice.) "We decided not to buy the yacht this year."

"What does your husband do for a living?" "He prays a lot. God will provide. Look what he's done for us so far! We're living proof!" (If there's one that gets 'em, this one does!)

"How are you going to provide for all of them?

College is so expensive." "We're going to do the best we can, just as our parents did for us, and the rest we'll leave to God's planning."

We wouldn't be here today if it weren't for our parents and grandparents, who made it through wars, depression periods, unemployment and hard times yet still welcomed *us* into their homes and hearts. In this affluent age can we seriously suggest that not having provision for four years of college should deny a child a chance for life? As our priests used to say, "God will provide." And he does.

"Aren't you worried about overpopulation?" "No, we're more concerned about *underpopulation,* which according to the United States Census Bureau is a *real* problem. We're doing *our* part!"

"Aren't you concerned about the earth and the environment?" "No, my concern is to live the way God calls me to live. We have an obligation to be good stewards of this land, but God wants us to welcome and rejoice when he blesses us with new life: the crowning jewel of his creation."

This one is hard on the "earth people," who have all but lost sight of the reason for God's creation and of the fact that children are our greatest natural resource!

> So God created humankind in his image,
>> in the image of God he created them;
>> male and female he created them.
>
> God blessed them, and God said to them, "Be fruitful and multiply, and fill the earth and subdue it; and have dominion over the fish of the sea and over the birds of the air and over every living thing that moves upon the earth." God said, "See, I have given you every plant yielding seed that is upon the face of all the earth, and every tree with seed in its fruit;

you shall have them for food. And to every beast of
the earth, and to every bird of the air, and to everything that creeps on the earth, everything that has
the breath of life, I have given every green plant
for food."

—GENESIS 1:27–30

This last question is more fun to answer with each baby:
"Now, is this IT for you?" "Oh, no! We're just getting
started."

As John and I learned firsthand, God is *never* outdone
in generosity. In other words, no matter the cynicism or
criticism, the "best is yet to be!" 🌳

Whoever welcomes one such child in my name
welcomes me.

—MATTHEW 18:5

6

The Gift of Love

I remember a conversation from years ago between my then five-year-old son, Tim, and his newly adopted brother. Charlie had come from an orphanage in Vietnam and had probably experienced more sadness, separation and death than most American adults will ever know, as evidenced by his nightmares and unfounded fears. Miraculously he was settling into our family fairly well and, after a few months of tutoring, was quickly picking up the English language.

Charlie and Tim were sitting at the kitchen table, quietly coloring pictures as I prepared dinner nearby. Looking forward to Charlie's first birthday with our family, Tim was curious about what life was like for Charlie before his arrival.

"What kind of birthday presents did you get at your other house?" Tim asked Charlie.

"What's a present?" Charlie asked.

Tim's eyes widened. "You know, gifts! Toys and stuff to play with!"

Charlie looked puzzled. "I never had any."

In persistent disbelief Tim asked, "You mean you *never* had a birthday party?"

"Nope."

"No presents? Ever?"

"Nope."

"Well then, how did you get to be five?"

"Me don't know. Me just kept growing!"

Charlie was right. Despite the poverty, the war and the uncertainty of his future, he kept growing! The primary reason was because he *felt* loved from the very beginning. His birth mother, though alone and poor, cared for him. Only later, when she feared for his safety and well-being because of the downfall of Saigon to communism, did she entrust Charlie to a Catholic priest, who brought him to the orphanage for care.

Charlie's arrival in our home reminded us anew of how vital love is to a youngster's life. He had experienced war, bombings, hunger, sickness, deaths of loved ones and even the separation from his own mother, yet he was a survivor because he felt loved.

Contrast that with Tony's experience. He came from Vietnam on a special emergency medical visa during the Christmas season. He was two months old and weighed a scant five pounds. On the papers handed to us at the airport was typed, "Child will not survive orphanage life."

The statistics coming from Vietnam and Cambodia during the war years disclosed that 80 percent of infants under one year died. The reason was not lack of nutrition; there were milk and formula supplies going in even during the war. Rather, the explanation for the high death rates was a "lack of stimulation." The missing ingredient for the orphaned infants was holding, hugging and love! It takes only a matter of months for infants who are never held to become lethargic and apathetic. Ultimately they lose their will to live.

Tony's first three months in our home were fragile, with more than his share of doctor and emergency room visits. Here was a child who never cried—not a peep, *ever!* That in itself would disarm any good mother!

During the day I would strap him to me as I went about my daily chores and cared for our other three children (all under five). At night we would place Tony in a baby buggy next to our bed so we could monitor his breathing. Some nights I could only fall asleep with my hand resting on his back to feel the rhythm of his breathing.

Ultimately Tony, too, was a survivor. We credit the quick action of the orphanage and the goodwill of the American government, which granted the visa that saved him from the fate to which so many other infants his age were left.

Today both Charlie and Tony are grown and living on their own. They're fine young men with no trace of their early struggles.

We learned from Charlie and Tony and our other adopted children that sometimes children can have lots of *things* yet be virtually starving for the only things in life that really matter: security, permanence and *LOVE*. And love can take hold and grow only when security and permanence are the foundation.

We also learned that *nothing*—no well-supplied orphanage, no state-of-the-art day care and no well-trained caregiver—can take the place of parental love and, better still, the full-time presence of a mother. Children have an uncanny sense of knowing when they are—or are *not*—top priority!

Unlike millions around the globe who struggle to stay alive and together in spite of regional wars, oppressive governments, famine or hardship, American families are blessed to live in a nation of peace and prosperity. We are free to live our faith and share our dreams within what Pope John Paul II called the *"sanctuary* of the family." Yet America is a nation that leads the world in childhood depression and addictions. How can that be?

Mother Teresa said that "America is the poorest of nations" because we reject our young—over 1.3 million infants each year—with legalized abortion. It is that attitude of callous disregard, she says, that permeates and poisons an entire society.

Symptoms of such poverty of spirit are evident in the cases of child neglect and abuse, rates of which have risen 400 percent since abortion was legalized. That is the bad news.

But there is good news evident in our Catholic faith. We look at the strong leadership Pope John Paul II provided in this area. He wrote and spoke eloquently on the vital role of family and the blessings of children. His encyclical *The Gospel of Life* says, "The family has a special role to play…from birth to death. It is truly 'the *sanctuary of life*: the place in which life—the gift of God—can be properly welcomed and protected against the many attacks to which it is exposed and can develop in accordance with what constitutes authentic human growth'" (*The Gospel of Life*, 92).[1]

More good news is the millions of couples who strive to live out the gospel of life. They are open and obedient to God's will, viewing their children as gifts, welcoming each one—the planned and the "surprises"—as God's blessing! In America they live in a counterculture, embracing selflessness and sacrifice for the good of others. But in the end they will experience treasures that those caught in the world of "me first" never will. There is freedom and joy in living as God calls us to live.

I will concede that parenting—especially parenting a large family—is not always easy. But the blessings far exceed the burdens. The old adage is true: God is never outdone in generosity. When you care for his babies, he will take good care of you! 🌳

7

Unsung Heroines

I was struck by a recent *New York Times* article about a young naval commander, in charge of a guided missile destroyer, who was preparing to head out to sea. The headline read, "In command on shore and at sea," and the story described a thirty-nine-year-old officer who is "a rarity in the Navy": a woman in command of a warship.

But it was the accompanying photo that really tugged at my heart. The woman commander had a young toddler draped across her arms. As my kids would say, "What's wrong with this picture?"

The article described in glowing terms a "39-year-old, 5-foot mother with a determined swagger" and her "ability to take the helm of the large warship and its 300-member crew as it headed to sea."[1] It failed to mention, however, *who* would be "in command on shore," taking care of her child or children while she is on her six-month watch at sea with the United States Navy.

Are we so turned around as a society that it is now more noble and noteworthy for a woman to leave home to serve in battle than to nurture and care for the souls entrusted to her by God, her own children?

The naval commander story reminded me of another woman in the news. She serves her state as lieutenant governor, and she took time from her official duties long enough to give birth to twins before going back on the job. She recently announced her bid to run for governor. Obviously this mother believes the citizens of her state need her more than her babies. Time will tell.

In my hometown a local newscaster offered evening viewers a "unique insight" into her first-time pregnancy, taking her audience along (via camera crew) on doctor visits and ultrasound tests. As the event drew closer, she collected donations of baby items in honor of her little one, to later be given to needy families in the community. After all the fanfare and a mere ten days after her baby's birth, she was back at the anchor desk reporting the evening news, looking trim and slim. Gossip columnists attributed the quick on-the-job-return to her fear of missing the "news sweep" polls, which could cut into her popularity with the public.

If only such competitive moms, who feel the call of career more than child, could understand a few simple life lessons:

- Children have an uncanny sense of *knowing* if they or something else have top priority.

- Time is of the essence. A woman can always resume or pursue a career. Millions do it every day. But this is your one shot, one time and one opportunity to be with your child.

- Love really is a four-letter word spelled *t-i-m-e:* "I love you enough to give you my time." A sense of bonding and belonging is guaranteed *only* when a child receives "quantity time," not the "quality time" that some espouse.

These dressed-for-success mothers are a far cry from the ones I know. The young moms I know may never receive an award or even honorable mention. They may never win an election or cause the stock exchange to go up or down. You probably will never read about them in *The New York Times* or see them showcased in *People* magazine. They will command no ship, make no speeches and never head a socially select committee of distinction. And probably the only decoration on their shoulders will be diapers or baby spit-up.

These women, by God's grace, have chosen to put the care of their husbands and children *first*.

This choice may not be valued or recognized by society's standards, but truly these women are, as more than one president has stated, the very "backbone" of our great nation. They are raising God's babies and America's greatest natural resource!

The church sees motherhood as a vocational call from God. Here's what Pope John Paul II had to say about women who hear the call and accept it:

> It is in [the context of daily living], so humanly rich and filled with love, that *heroic actions* too are born. These are the *most solemn celebration of the Gospel of life*, for they proclaim it by the *total gift of self*. They are the radiant manifestation of the highest degree of love, which is to give one's life for the person loved (cf. Jn 15:13). They are sharing in the mystery of the Cross…. There is an everyday heroism, made up of gestures of sharing, big or small, which build up an authentic culture of life….
>
> Part of this daily heroism is the silent but effective and eloquent witness of all those "brave mothers who devote themselves to their own family without reserve, who suffer in giving birth to their children

and who are ready to make any effort, to face any sacrifice, in order to pass on to them the best of themselves."

In living out their mission "these heroic women do not always find support in the world around them. On the contrary, the cultural models frequently promoted and broadcast by the media do not encourage motherhood. In the name of progress and modernity the values of fidelity, chastity, sacrifice, to which a host of Christian wives and mothers have borne and continue to bear outstanding witness, are presented as obsolete.... We thank you, heroic mothers, for your invincible love! We thank you for your intrepid trust in God and in his love. We thank you for the sacrifice of your life.... In the Paschal Mystery, Christ restores to you the gift you gave him. Indeed, he has the power to give you back the life you gave him as an offering." (*Gospel of Life*, 86, emphasis mine)[2]

In other words, we may never be heroines in the eyes of the secular world, but our faith teaches that mothers who love unconditionally—putting the care of their husbands, home and children over unnecessary outside career goals—are truly living God's vocational call to holiness. It's something to keep in mind on days when we feel like throwing in the dish towel for something more glamorous! 🌳

No good thing does the LORD withhold
from those who walk uprightly.

—PSALM 84:11

8

What's It Like in a BIG Family?

Not long ago a young woman approached me as I was shopping and asked, "Aren't you Mrs. Kuharski?"

When I said, "Yes," an instant conversation began.

"I used to go to school with one of your daughters," the young woman said. "In fact, I remember being at your house for a couple of Theresa's birthday parties."

She spoke of her engagement and impending marriage, as well as her future hopes to be a stay-at-home mom "with lots of kids." I wasn't sure where this was going, but it sure beat the "career first" monologues I usually heard.

"I'll never forget what it was like the first time I was at your house," this pretty and petite young woman continued. "Coming from a small family, I couldn't believe all the kids under *one* roof! They were coming in, going out, on the phone and at the door, *all* chattering nonstop. I thought to myself, 'This is the craziest place I've ever seen.... And it's *exactly* what I want to have someday!'"

"You're sure you mean *my* family?" I responded.

The young woman was sure. She had come away from those visits with some kind of starry-eyed notion that we actually had fun living like that! And she's right.

Granted, big family life is not for everyone. But then

neither is getting married, joining a cloistered convent, bungee jumping or signing up for desert duty with the French Foreign Legion.

"What's it like living in a *big* family?" people often ask me.

"It's like a never-ending soup kitchen," I'm sometimes tempted to answer. But in truth I can't imagine life any other way!

Admittedly there is little silence, space or solitude. At our house there's *always* somebody around to talk, play, fight, discuss, share, consult or just *be* with. And on those rare occasions when you are home alone, the quiet is so awkward that you find yourself *waiting* for someone to come through the door and create some noise!

"Hey, where is everybody?" Dominic asked one evening at dinner, when he and Joseph were the only kids at the table. "This is spooky!" Thanks.

So what's it like in a big family? Well, here are some of the quirks we've come to accept as part of our life:

✎ In a big family parents can lie in bed in the morning and hear discussions such as "Who took *all* the sweet cereal?" "How come you *always* get the prize!" "Who drank all the juice?" "Did you take my bagel? It had *my* name on it." "You're wearing my top. You could have at least *asked*." "Who took the last slice of pizza? Mom said it was for *me*." "I wish we could have ice cream for breakfast like Andy!" (Hmmmm.)

✎ In big families, my grandma used to say, "The first one up is the best one fed and dressed!" She was right.

✐ Big families invented the word *conservation*. From bathrooms and bedrooms to bikes and baseballs, to beach towels and book bags, most *everything* is shared, "handed down" or recycled.

✐ "Time-share" in our world does NOT mean a condo in Florida. Rather it's the minutes you're allotted to use the phone, bathroom, shower, hair dryer, microwave, computer and even the iron and laundry room. Time is precious, especially when someone is waiting for his or her turn.

✐ *Preservation* is another big-family "buzzword." Its telltale signs can be seen in watered-down juice, ketchup and salad dressings. (No one at our house is quite sure what Thousand Island dressing or fruit punch really tastes like.) The soap dishes hold little bits of soap chips smashed together so that every last sliver can be used.

✐ At our house the sweet cereal is mixed with the plain, and bread crusts are never given to the birds. We eat more bread and veggies than meat. "It's better for you," we tell our kids. "He grants peace within your borders; he fills you with the finest of wheat" (Psalm 147:14).

✐ There are no thieves in big families, just hungry kids. It's not unusual to find a new box of cookies, crackers or cereal with only bits and crumbs remaining. The juice container in the fridge doesn't have enough liquid left to fill a parakeet's eyedropper. Then there's the ice cream bucket in the freezer (pints and quarts are nonexistent) with less than a teaspoonful at the bottom. On occasion we've found the scoop lying in the bottom of the bucket, the obvious sign of someone's hasty getaway!

- *No one* ever "takes the last one." Who wants to have to answer to "Who ate the last ice cream bar?" Or cracker or cookie—notice it's never green beans!

- Someone may remove a frozen pizza or baked goods from the freezer but leave the container undisturbed. This is perhaps done, as one of my clever sons suggested, "so the freezer won't fill up with frost." What can I say?

- Freshly baked *anything* (burnt and all) disappears without ever making it to the cookie jar, table or freezer. I store my Christmas cookies in a bedroom closet; John keeps the soda pop and microwave popcorn under his bedroom dresser.

- Open the refrigerator on any given day, and you're likely to find labels taped to leftover storage containers, bearing someone's name or simply, "Don't Touch," "Don't Eat" or "Please Save," instructions that are usually ignored.

- Common phrases in big families are "Wait your turn," "I was here first," "Move over," "This is *my* spot!" (Children in big families don't have rooms; they claim "spots.") "No fair," "How come Mom let you? She never lets me," "You do, and I'll tell!" "It's not my job!" "It's not my turn!" and "Why me? I did it last time!"

Now, you might say that you hear these comments in small families too, but I bet I hear more of them!

Yes, members of big families do bicker and borrow without asking. But it's been my observation that times of ill content are few and fleeting. What my husband and I marvel at most is the caring, the companionship and the genuine, honest-to-goodness "No, you go first" love that we see in our young.

One day, for example, Kari and Angie, then in their early teens, were locked in a heated argument that had no apparent solution. Finally one looked at the other and said, "Soooooo, let's do something else."

"OK," the other answered, and off they went.

When our son Tony entered the army, he mentioned that he came from a family of thirteen. His drill sergeant remarked, "That's what we like to hear. You'll do great in the infantry. Guys from big families are used to rules, discipline, obeying orders, sharing and looking out for others." And here our Tony thought he was getting away from all that!

Big families learn the meaning of sacrifice by osmosis, doing without and sharing with others. They understand patience and persistence at close range, not to mention the skill of dealing with multiple personalities "with minds of their own." Whether they're home around the kitchen table, doing chores or playing on the beach, big families have a closeness and camaraderie that is a blessing all its own.

What else but love could explain the other kind of phrases we hear: "Do you need some help?" "It's OK. I don't mind." "Here, use mine!" "I'm sorry I hurt you." "Wanna play?" "You're a good bud." "Are you feeling better? I prayed for you last night." "Want some help with that homework?" "I'll help you with that, and you can help me with this. We'll be done quicker!"

"Be kind to one another, compassionate, and mutually forgiving, just as God has forgiven you in Christ" (Ephesians 4:32).

"The family," Pope John Paul II often reminded us, is the "domestic church."[1] It is in the home and at the kitchen table that our children are first exposed to love and faith.

Big families, then, are probably not much different from small ones; our "congregations" are just larger. With prayer and God's grace, we see the power of his love every day. What a pity that the population zealots, who promote "small if at all," and the couples who are childless by choice will never experience the goodness of what my daughter's friend sensed so intensely.

> How very good and pleasant it is
>   when kindred live together in unity!
>
> —PSALM 133:1

9

Favorite Memories
of Mom

The spring and summer of 2004 brought its usual array of family gatherings. We celebrated birthdays, graduations, piano recitals and kindergarten "roundups" for grandchildren.

In addition we celebrated the wedding of our daughter Angela (number nine) to her chosen "prince," Adam Johnson. Those "in the know" on family weddings will tell you that things begin months in advance with shopping, showers, more shopping and more showers, all building to the excitement of the wedding day.

You'd think that would be enough parties and activities for this large family. But no, John and the kids hosted a huge surprise birthday party for me. And that it was: I was caught totally off guard.

As part of the surprise they invited guests to write a "favorite memory." That could have been embarrassing, if not dangerous. But actually it was a great idea and really a nostalgic look at some of the wonderful family, friends and events in my life. The little notes and photos are cherished reminders of those loved ones.

My kids came up with their own version of "favorite memories." They pasted it on the dining room wall for all to see. Maybe you want to share it with your own children. They'll know how good they have it with you once they see some of the rules this mom enforced!

What are our favorite memories of Mom?

- Is it how she wouldn't let us girls call boys on the telephone?

- Is it how we had a dishwasher in the house and never got to use it because, she said, "I have thirteen dishwashers!"

- Is it how EVERY year during Lent we HAD to give up watching television?

- Is it how we never were able to wear bikinis in the summer like everyone else?

- Or how our curfew was set at midnight, because "there is nothing good that happens after midnight"?

- Is it how we were only able to watch ONE hour of television a night?

- Or how we could never have sleepovers?

- Hearing Mom say when we woke up, "The first one up is the best one fed!" and discovering the only cereal left was the non-sugar ones?

- Is it the memories of family vacations: driving cross-country in one BIG van and sleeping in two hotel rooms (one for the boys and one for the girls)?

- Maybe it's the holiday family meals and the time Mom invited the lady who worked at Copy Max to join us for dinner.

- Or those "guilt-free" calls after we left home, when she'd call to remind us that "today is a holy day."

- Is it being woken up by Mom's singing, "Good morning to you, good morning to you. We're all in our places with bright shiny faces. And this is the way we start our new day"?

- The perms we ALL got (including Tim and our neighbor, Mr. A.)?

- Or is it the times we were out shopping for clothes and Mom would check the fit of our pants by grabbing our legs?

- How she always sang, "Hubba, Hubba, ding, ding, Baby, you got everything!" when we were all dressed up to go out (or in the dressing room at the store)?

- How we couldn't get our ears pierced until we were sixteen and couldn't walk out of the house with holes in our jeans?

- And when we asked, "Where are you going?" she'd reply, "Crazy. Want to come along?"

- How she "uses" us kids and our family experiences in her articles and books?

- How she calls all of our friends "honey," no matter who they are, because she can't remember their names?

- Is it how she's ALWAYS losing things (and keeping poor Saint Anthony busy by praying for their appearance)?

- How we ALWAYS sat in the front row at church, even though we were ALWAYS the last to arrive? She said it kept our attention.

- How she's always soooo SHY in sharing her opinions with others (wink, wink)?

Even though we seldom admit it, we do love Mom for all of the reasons above and more. But mostly we love Mom for bringing us into this world (each of us in a different way), for showing us the importance of our faith, giving us each other and demonstrating to us unconditional love through the example she sets every day.

Love from your kids.

> Her children rise up and call her happy.
> —PROVERBS 31:28

10

Taking Toddlers to Church

A young couple in my parish who attend Mass with their four children every Sunday received a letter from an anonymous parishioner complaining about the distraction their little ones were causing during the liturgy. What a shame! Wasn't it Christ who said, "Let the little children come unto me"?

I know the young family who received the note. In fact, I've never witnessed, in the years I've sat behind this family, a tantrum, outburst or distractive misbehavior from their children. Occasionally one of their young may cry out or need a bathroom break that won't wait, but the mother or father always leaves quietly and with little notice. In my view, either the anonymous writer targeted the wrong family, is supersensitive to *any* disturbance or was just having a bad day and yearned for an hour of solitude and serenity to talk to the Lord.

We must remember that Sunday Mass is not meant to be a solo service or personal retreat but a liturgy involving the entire church community. And that includes children.

Christians are supposed to be people of faith and joy. We know that each little baby is made in God's own image and likeness, and each is part of his perfect plan. If we don't welcome and celebrate God's precious gift of new life—including an occasional outburst—who will? Certainly not the unchurched or the "culture of death" folks, whose "right" to legal abortion claims the lives of nearly forty-four hundred babies each day.

Don't get me wrong. I'm all for keeping church pews as prayerful and peaceful as possible. I get as agitated as the anonymous writer when I see parents do absolutely nothing while their small children act up. Frankly, I have all I can do to keep from going over and offering to *help* them be parents!

But there are times when, in spite of every effort and preparation, a little one's outburst or crankiness can't be helped. In that case parents need to take their young disturbance out as quickly and quietly as possible. Certainly God will bless such parents for their prayerful effort.

This is one "seasoned mom" who has probably spent more time than most parents standing in vestibules, rocking fussy infants or calming antsy toddlers. The only thing that seemed to keep many of our colicky newborns quiet was motion, which meant I often made a quick exit from our place in the front pew and walked or rocked them in the back of the church through the remainder of the service.

Yet John and I understood the importance of attending Mass together as a family. We realized that the most important lesson of faith we could instill in our children is not what we tell them but what they see. I am convinced that the most powerful witness a child can see is his or her parents—especially the father—kneeling in prayer, in reverence and awe for our great and powerful heavenly Father!

As for those of us who have no small children to care for, let us praise God for the gift these little ones and their families are to our community. Let us pray for them. And let us pray especially for people in our world who have lost their sense of the miraculous and are blind to the gift God has placed in our presence, some of whom are only inches tall and have a set of lungs that could match those of an opera star!

Here are some practical tips that helped us get through Mass peacefully when our children were small:

- Be prepared for baby's needs. If you are bringing an infant to church, bring bottles, a pacifier, diapers and a bib. If you're a nursing mom, put away those one-piece dresses and wear skirts and tops that can be easily adjusted. Find a chair in the back of the church or in a separate room if feeding is a noticeable disruption.

- For the restless infant or toddler, small, *quiet* toys are appropriate time-passers.

- Prepare preschoolers. Making sure your children have a good breakfast and *always* go to the bathroom just before leaving home keeps disruptions to a minimum. Some youngsters fuss simply because they are hungry.

- As for the bathroom, when in doubt, take them out! Some children truly can't wait one more minute.

- Wear your Sunday best. Children, even the very young, comprehend the importance of an occasion by the way we dress and prepare. Sunday clothes don't have to be new and expensive, but they should be something special, acknowledging the One we are coming to visit.

✐ Teens and young adults may need to be reminded of the importance of modesty, especially when coming to church. Many parishes have found it necessary to post signs in vestibules or in church bulletins stating, "No shorts, halters or sleeveless tops."

✐ Sit up front. Most children behave better when they are seated near the front and can see the altar and priest.

✐ Trust me on this one. Try the front row for six weeks, and see if your wriggly youngster is not transformed into a quiet, attentive observer. Of course, there may still be times when you have to remove a cranky kid from the congregation so that others may pray in peace.

✐ Don't be discouraged. God will bless your effort. Saint Augustine held that the sincere intent to pray is a prayer.[1] Just be sure to offer your morning and your attendance at Mass as a prayer, and it is a pleasing gift to God. Your weekly persistence will eventually pay off. Children are the greatest imitators, and soon enough they will kneel and pray just as they see you do.

✐ Bring children's books. Small booklets of faith with colorful pictures and easily understood language are perfect for young churchgoers. Save these items for church use only so the child will look forward to using them, or have several selections and rotate their use.

🖎 Know what to avoid. Don't bring large dolls, trucks or noisy items for children. And *please,* no gum or messy food or candy.

🖎 Expect good behavior. Children need to learn that there are some occasions during which they must be quiet and refrain from talk or play. This is a good manners-and-discipline builder. Insist the child try, but don't expect perfection. Patience and persistence are key!

🖎 Yes, it takes practice, but even the very young are eager to please and to copy the actions of others—especially their parents and family. Praising a child for being good goes a long way toward reinforcing the behavior.

🖎 Encourage your children to participate. Lovingly remind them that *no* prayer is too small and *no* child too young to get God's attention. The simple act of blessing themselves with holy water, genuflecting, lighting a candle and saying a short prayer for a loved one or placing the envelope in the collection lets them feel they are part of the liturgy.

🖎 Make Sunday special. Our heavenly Father rested on Sunday and commands us to do the same. It's up to us as parents to let our children know from an early age that God and family come first, especially on Sunday!

11

Married to the Coupon King

I should have read the signs when we were dating, but frankly I thought it was kind of cute when John would pull out a coupon for a "half-off" dinner or a "two-for-the-price-of-one" movie ticket. Little did I dream.

After we married, I quickly came to realize that it was no mere coincidence when John knew of a discount or just "happened to have" a coupon handy. No, frugality was part of his makeup.

Perhaps he acquired this trait from his wonderful Polish mother, whose frugality was a family legend. She was the only woman I ever knew who routinely washed out bottles, jars and milk cartons for reuse and who stored her leftovers in rewashed plastic bags. When a clothing item became threadbare, she would save the buttons, snaps and sometimes even the zipper to use again. If the thread from a garment's hem was salvageable, she pulled and re-spooled it. Nothing was wasted or discarded. Her kids called her "the original recycler."

John's mother picked up these habits during the Depression years. She felt that they would be good for all Americans to adopt. Judging by the clutter and debris lining our streets and highways, not to mention our overflowing trash bins, I think she was right. Conservation and protection of our environment is a small way of showing our gratitude to a gracious God who gave us the whole world.

I frankly think that John and his mother's recycling habits had more to do with their strong Catholic upbringing than with anything else. Catholics have a tradition of treating *all* things as gifts from God's creative hand. When we were young, we were taught respect for our environment, and to waste or abuse things given to us was sinful. Thus the good sisters in Catholic schools taught that a piece of paper with writing on one side should be turned over to the other side for use as scratch paper.

I don't know for sure if John's frugality is an inherited trait or merely a skill he has honed with time and now perfected to a "science." What I do know is that where John is involved there has never been a purchase—including the materials for our renovated bathrooms, the outdoor siding, our automobiles and Joseph's eighth-grade graduation shoes—that didn't come about as a result of a coupon, bargain or one of John's deals.

I might mention here that some of his "deals" have been costly disasters. For example, he insisted that the car he bought at a used car auction "just needs a little tune-up and work." He had to junk it after the transmission blew. But that's another story!

I love bargains too, and it's no secret that I shop garage sales and thrift stores. When the kids were young, I gladly accepted all the "nearly new" clothes passed our way. This was not only sensible; the kids often enjoyed wearing an item once worn by a neighbor or older sibling.

To save money I became the family barber—and a pretty good one. Well, there was the one time I got distracted and clipped a chunk of hair off the back of Charlie's head. I had to color it over with magic marker so it wasn't noticeable when he served Mass the next morning.

But all in all, I'm no match for John.

People often ask how we managed to raise thirteen children on *one* salary. They don't know John. Mr. Budget can make a dollar stretch further than a magician. He delights in knowing his frugality has outwitted those gloomy prognosticators who predict that "it takes $180,000 to raise one child to age eighteen."

"Not if you start 'em early on paper routes, lawn and shoveling jobs, baby-sitting and saving pop cans for recycling," John says.

We affectionately call him the "Coupon King," a label applied even outside the family. One of our neighbors could think of no better Christmas gift for John than a sleek black coupon wallet—complete with dividers and a Velcro snap—to hold his stash. John takes great delight in coming home with a grocery receipt that displays a running total of coupon credits equal to—if not greater than—his total purchase amount.

But his frugality extends way beyond groceries. When son Michael (eighteen) saw what I was writing, he said, "Tell 'em how he uses aerosol spray paint, duct tape or Bondo to cover up chips, rust or cracks so we don't think we need something new." True. We find traces of John's "repairs" on everything from old bikes, toys, cars and boats to lamps, yard furniture and metal file cabinets. We took a suitcase on vacation once, only to discover, when we arrived at our destination, a gaping hole in the top of the case where John had applied a hefty portion of Bondo.

Don't get me wrong, John enjoys life, loves a good time and adores his children and grandchildren. This is a man who spends hours in the November cold putting up a Christmas display of over fifteen thousand twinkling lights and more figurines than I can count or describe—all for the delight of children. That's on the outside of the house. On the inside he is on his normal vigil of shutting off lights "we don't need," turning down the thermostat and telling me to "put on a sweater if you're so cold."

Tim, one of our older sons, recently told a coworker, "When we were young, my Dad's idea of taking us to lunch was loading us in the van on Saturday morning (I only heard of this later) and going through the free sample lines at the supermarket or getting free hot dogs and chips at a car dealership." (Of course, he never bought the car!)

John's newest hobby is auctions. I suppose I should be thankful he's not a smoker, drinker, gambler or "chaser" (as my mother would say), but the guy is now *hooked* on the thrill of holding up a little card with a number on it and getting a great price for a boxful of something we don't need.

His recent take-homes include a two-foot wooden owl, which he spray-painted a metallic gold and I promptly banished to a corner of the backyard, an over-sized sculpted cast-iron cat, various glassware (none of which I can use) and a birdhouse that is not fit for outdoor use. Most of it John obtained for fewer than five dollars, he quickly reminds me. He's convinced that there are at least a few things among the bargains that "someone can use."

I must say that when it comes to me and the children, John is *never* stingy but *always* generous with his time, attention and what matters most: his love and a deep sense of faith in a God who is never outdone in generosity. I have come to treasure John's thrifty ways and his big, generous heart. He has always managed to cut through the material distractions that could have blinded us to the true treasures of life, which came to us with smudgy hands and with faces and personalities that won our hearts and made the budgeting quite a bargain at that!

When I married my Polish prince, little did I dream that he would turn out to be a coupon king! But were it not for him, the thirteen "products of our love" would not be here today!

> Wealth and riches are in their houses,
> and their righteousness endures for ever.
>
> —PSALM 112:3

12

The Family That Plays Together, Stays Together!

John and I are big advocates of the annual family vacation. There's just nothing like it. Something magical occurs when parents and children put *everything* on hold and take time away to *play!* Going out to eat, a day at the park or zoo is nice, but nothing beats packing up the car and getting away from the phones, schedules and, yes, even friends, to be together for recreation and rest.

Even soldiers in the midst of war are encouraged to take a break and get away for a few days of "R&R," as the army calls it. We on the home front should do no less. "An investment in our family" is what my accountant husband calls it. "It's worth the time and money," he reasoned, when we had more time than money. "Before we know it, everyone will be grown and on their own. We need to do it now."

Yes, we vacationed even when we couldn't afford to. "We can't afford not to" was our reasoning. We all shared in the financial sacrifice. The children took paper routes, baby-sat, mowed lawns and recycled aluminum cans in order to make our annual goal a reality. Well worth the effort!

A family vacation is a wonderful way to bond and create memories that will last a lifetime, memories that are so vital in our family-fractured society. What better way to explore the countryside and see the bountiful beauty of God's creation than to do it together?

During the early years our sense of adventure took us no farther than the peaceful though cramped quarters of Grandma's cabin at Clearwater Lake in Annandale, Minnesota. This was a haven for our crew and a piece of heaven for their parents—seeing them all enjoy the outdoors and just be kids! They learned to fish, swim and water ski. They boasted an annual collection of toads, turtles, tadpoles and bugs second to none!

They also accumulated more than their share of leeches, wood ticks, poison ivy and poison oak. Even the challenges of spotting and treating these brought shared laughter and memories!

Then we got braver. Soon we were packing our van and heading for places far and wide, such as the Black Hills of South Dakota, Colorado, Pennsylvania, Kentucky, Missouri and Washington, D.C. Our all-time biggest feat was a fifty-four-hundred-mile trek to California and back, an "adventure" with ten children.

Those were the days when we could squeeze everyone into one van. We also got by with one motel room. (God bless those motel owners!) The thumb-suckers in diapers slept in sleeping bags on the floor, while the two beds were reserved: one for John and me and the other for girls one night and boys the next. Their bed was crowded, of course, but I can still hear the snickers and giggles. Thankfully we couldn't afford luxury suites. We would have missed the memories.

As the children grew in age and size, we needed a minimum of two cars and two motel rooms. John headed up a room for the boys, and I one for the girls.

Of course, some of those "memories" take a little distance and time before our sense of humor kicks in and we can appreciate them. On our trip to Colorado, we almost turned around and headed home. One of our colicky babies screamed at full volume as we attempted to navigate our way down a narrow mountain road. The swimming pool and the pizza in our room later saved the day.

And then there was the hot summer day when we all craved ice cream cones. We picked up the supplies at a grocery store along the way. Then Theresa, in her rush to get a coveted seat by the window, left the bag of ice cream in the parking lot. We only discovered the loss when we stopped miles down the road for our picnic lunch.

Just keeping track of everyone was a challenge. We lost Michael at Wall Drug in South Dakota. The whole family was in a state of panic, while he sat perched on a countertop, refusing to give his name and quietly enjoying a huge sucker given to him by one of the employees.

On one trip we were five miles out of a little mountain town in Colorado, where we had refueled, when we remembered to tell the kids to "count off." Only then did we realize that Tina was not in the count. We rushed back to the gas station. She had slipped away to buy a candy bar as we were loading up. Needless to say, the candy was immediately confiscated as a reminder that "we stay together!"

I won't even mention all the times we were stranded in remote areas (such as the Mojave Desert) because of car trouble, or the emergency room trips we made for high fevers, pierced eardrums, stitches and broken collarbones! These are just a given in family life.

Then there are the little annoyances. "We're bonding," some of my teens would remind me when I blew my top over soggy clothes in a suitcase, the result of someone's stuffing in a wet suit or towel the day before.

The best protection and security I know of for a great family vacation is to pray the rosary daily. The car ride is the best time for this. There's nothing like a captive audience!

Daily Mass is a blessing all its own. Our family has ·fond memories of the wonderful priests and people we encountered simply because we included Mass as part of our vacation. There were unforgettable churches as well, such as the small Indian mission in Arizona where our boys were invited to be altar servers and the unconsecrated hosts were stored in a margarine container.

There's just something about sharing together in the adventure and even the aggravations that are sure to occur on an all-family trip. So wonderful were those times together that even now the Kuharski family has its annual vacation, including adult children and grandchildren and a caravan of cars.

> You shall go out in joy,
>   and be led back in peace;
> the mountains and the hills before you
>   shall burst into song,
>   and all the trees of the field shall clap their hands.
> —Isaiah 55:12

13

Boys and Their Toys

All your children shall be taught by the Lord,
and great shall be the prosperity of your children.
—ISAIAH 54:13

I remember the year Chrissy, our oldest daughter, bounded through the back door and took me aside to ask, "Do you think Dad is OK? I mean, has he kind of flipped out or something?" As she spoke, a tow truck was dropping the remains of a badly rusted car in our driveway, as John looked on with eager anticipation.

"Why would Dad want something like *that*? It's ugly and doesn't even run," she asked.

"That's exactly *why* he wants it," I explained. "You see, Chrissy, men are simply grown-up little boys, and most of the ones I know have a hobby, a sport or some sort of toy. For Dad and your brothers, this is theirs."

Once the delivery of the old car and assorted parts was complete, John and our then-teenage boys—Tim, Charlie and Tony—slipped on their oldest clothes and began to work on their new "project." It took them better than a year to repair, rebuild and restore what I occasionally referred to as "that heap of scrap metal piled up in the driveway." Step by step they worked together, with John patiently instructing along the way. And when they were finished, they proudly displayed their prize: a blazing red Pontiac GTO with "four on the floor," a 400 engine and bucket seats!

The GTO became one of several "rebuilds" that John and our boys tackled. I must concede that it took me a while to develop an appreciation for what he was doing. But as I watched our teenagers come home from school, change into their "grubs," wolf down a snack and head for the garage, I began to see the positives.

First and foremost, it kept them busy. And with healthy adolescent boys that's more than a plus.

Second, the car held their interest, allowing few outside distractions. For instance, one of our high school sons was being heavily pursued by a young woman I'll call Brenda. He would hardly make it through the back door after school before the phone was ringing, and Brenda was purring his name on the other end of the line. Naturally he was flattered—at first. But it wasn't long before the attraction lost hold.

"I can't talk now. I'm busy. I'll see you in school," he'd quickly say. Then he was out in the driveway with his brothers and the GTO. Poor Brenda lost out to a rebuilt fender and a set of polished chrome hubcaps.

Third, the car project offered an outlet for some of our boys who didn't make the team or the grade or found themselves grounded for "unacceptable behavior," as the psychologists like to say. (One of our grounded kids could have rebuilt a 747 jet, but that's another story!)

Yes, John was more than right on this one. There's nothing like pounding out a tough piece of metal, rubbing down a bad rust spot or polishing up old chrome to take out an adolescent's frustrations.

Last and most importantly, the project built on something far more precious than a GTO: the love between a father and his sons. There was more than mechanics going on there, as our boys shared in the enthusiasm and the grime and grease (any mother with a washing machine can't help but notice) of rebuilding an old car. They were enjoying something precious and learning along the way—about diligence, discipline and determination—from the best teacher they could have: a dad who loves them.

"The father makes known to the children thy faithfulness" (Isaiah 38:19).

Sad to say, millions of young boys in America today would give almost anything to have the same opportunity. Statistics state that almost four out of ten American children do not live with their biological fathers.[1] According to the National Center for Fathering, only about half of today's children can expect to spend their entire childhood with an intact family.[2]

What that means is that millions of little boys may have no father image to look up to and emulate. And millions of little girls have no good father figure to look to as they mature and seek husbands who will one day be dads to their own children.

These statistics are in stark contrast to just a few decades ago, when 70 to 80 percent of young people lived at home with both parents. We may not be able to turn back the clock, but as Christians there *are* things we can do.

First, we can reach out to shattered families in prayer, asking Christ to become "the missing spouse" in those single-parent households.

Next, we can offer encouragement and support to the single moms we know. When possible we can help provide positive male role models for their youngsters. These moms must feel overwhelmed at times, trying to be both provider and nurturer. The same must be said for single fathers, who may not be as large a statistic but are nonetheless real.

Those of us blessed to be in an intact family can be grateful. And we can pray for God's grace and protection in an age that has little regard for what we know is Christ's "domestic church": the family!

As for the Kuharskis, one project seems to have led to another. I can always tell when John's getting ready for a new one. He walks in the back door with that look on his face. "I'm thinking of buying an old truck. I thought it would be a good project," he adds convincingly, "for Michael, Dominic and Joseph to help me with."

How can I say no?

As always, the truck is "a *real* steal!" (Some of his finds have come from those "drop off" places that take in donated vehicles for tax write-offs.) "All it needs is some engine and tune-up work, tires, a paint job, cleaning and fixing up on the interior. We'll have it running in no time!"

I can't wait!

Thank you, Lord, for the gift of fathers. Thank you for building your domestic church through their faithfulness and love! 🌲

14

The Rules Are
the Rules!

Your mother won't let you call boys?" our daughters' friends would ask. "What is she, from the Stone Age?"

"Just about," they'd grumble.

OK, so I'll never win the "Favorite Mother" or "My Mom's My Best Friend" award. So be it.

Our kids don't always appreciate our rules, especially when they enter the teen years. And I'm sure some didn't follow my advice once they were out of the house, at college or living on their own. But "while they live under our roof, the *rules* are the rules!"

A young mother once called and asked me to describe some of the rules John and I have regarding our teens and young adults. In a nutshell, here goes:

✐ No TVs in children's bedrooms. We have a family room, and that's where the entertainment and the family should be. No isolationists or loners allowed.

✐ I also control the programming and video-watching. No R-rated movies or other movies that I don't approve of. (The kids say that the Legion of Decency is more lenient.)

🖉 Curfews and going out with friends are contingent on good behavior, helpfulness around the house, the age of the child and schoolwork being complete.

🖉 No single dating before sixteen. This rule may seem archaic to some, but over the years we have not wavered on it, even when one or two of our "nearly sixteen" kids had to pass up a homecoming dance or special event. As "seasoned parents" we have found that responsibility and good decision-making come with age and maturity. Waiting until they are sixteen to date gives them not only something to look forward to but also time to prepare for and respect the responsibility of dating. Time is on our side.

🖉 A parent or supervising adult must be in the home when one of my kids is attending a party there or visiting the opposite sex. I have the prerogative to call and check. No matter how trustworthy the adolescent, the presence of a parent is the *only* and best insurance.

🖉 This is critical to a child's safety and reputation. Being in "the wrong place at the wrong time" causes many a young person misery when a party "gets out of hand" or property is broken or stolen and *everyone* involved becomes a suspect.

🖉 No dates on school nights. Teens need their rest. And parties and dates should not compromise the demands of school, extracurricular activities and part-time jobs.

🖉 No boys in girls' bedrooms or girls in boys' bedrooms. These areas are our private domain—where we sleep, where we dress and where our personal belongings are. They should not be for entertaining or visiting the opposite sex, which implies a not-so-subtle casualness and permissiveness.

✐ No lying together on sofas while watching TV and so on. The good nuns who taught me used to say we should *always* sit straight and keep the thickness of a phone book between us. (In Minneapolis that's two and a half inches!) We must never forget that temptation and the "near occasion of sin" are real.

✐ No tattoos or weird body piercings, no matter how chic, cute or trendy! Our bodies are temples of the Holy Spirit and belong to God.

✐ No bikinis (there's no such thing as a modest one!) or revealing two-piece swimsuits. Period! If I find evidence of one in our home (one returning college kid tried to sneak one in), it's trashed. This is our castle, and we have to answer for what we allow.

✐ No co-ed sleepovers or all-night parties—not on prom night or any other night. I don't care *who* promises to chaperone and stand vigil for the evening. When the night is over, our kids belong at home in their own beds.

✐ No motel or hotel overnights, and no spring breaks to faraway places—even with trusted chaperones. Teens and young adults do not *need* or *deserve* such a "getaway." (How many times have I heard well-intentioned parents make such an excuse?) Children should vacation with their families, not away from them!

✐ Enough accidents, illnesses and provocative enticements confront children every day without sending them off to exotic areas hours and miles away from us. Parents must never forget that *we* and no one else are responsible for the safety, well-being and protection of our children—teens and young adults included.

✐ Girls don't call boys. Let the boys do the pursuing and date planning. If he's interested, trust me, girls, he'll call. Young men enjoy being the pursuer and tire quickly of the female who seems too eager and available. Just ask our sons.

✐ Phone calls have limits: ten to twenty minutes per conversation. No phone calls after 9:00 P.M. for young children, 10:15 P.M. for young adults. College kids don't appreciate this time limit, but there must be consideration for the other members of the household and our need for privacy and sleep.

✐ Girls don't pay their own way or, worse, pay for the boy. The exception may be if they are engaged or attending an event as friends, with no romantic intention. "The only money you should have on a date," we've told our daughters, "is fifty cents to call home in case you need us."

✐ If finances are an issue, the boy needs to be more creative. Some of the most enjoyable dates are free or close to it: outdoor concerts; going to the zoo, a flower garden or a park; walking, biking, hiking or rollerblading; swimming and picnicking, to name a few.

✐ It goes without saying that we should teach our sons to treat a young woman to an enjoyable time *without* expecting any "favor" in return.

- Girls don't drive or pick up boys for dates. A young man should escort his date, picking her up at the door and meeting her parents before going out. No horn honking from the curb allowed. He should return her safely to her door at the end of the evening. It's old-fashioned, yes, but it sets the tone for the evening.

- This rule applies even if the girl lives farther from an event they are attending or has better "wheels." We must remember that a girl traveling alone at night, or stranded on the road, is a far more vulnerable target than a young man.

- Faith and family come first on Sundays. Father Patrick Peyton, founder of the Rosary Crusade, said it best: "The family that prays together, stays together." Begin your Sundays together in church. God is never outdone in generosity. What better witness than for our children to see *us* in prayer?

- Sunday dinners are also a time for the entire family to come together (unless outside jobs or special events prohibit it). Sharing an evening meal, especially on Sunday, is a comfortable way to keep everyone connected and informed about the happenings of the week, especially when there are varied ages and interests involved.

- Friends may come and go, but family is a gift from God. Let us take care to nurture and strengthen those bonds whenever possible. 🌳

I will instruct you and teach you the way you should go;
I will counsel you with my eye upon you.
—Psalm 32:8

15

Mom's Remedy for Naughty Talk

And whatever you do, in word or deed, do everything in the name of the Lord Jesus, giving thanks to God the Father through him.

—COLOSSIANS 3:17

I remember my jaw-dropping shock when I heard one of my little ones say a word that was downright vulgar. Unfortunately, with the number of kids in our family, this has happened more than once.

"Where did *that* come from?" I'd ask.

Most of the time they were too little to even understand the word or my shock. They were simply repeating what they had heard someone else say. Their response, if any, was, "Oh, I heard it on the playground," or "on the bus," "at the park," "from So-and-So."

Children are like sponges and mirrors. They absorb things quickly, and they reflect back what they see and hear. Most of the time we parents are grateful that they pick things up so fast. We hope that the faith and fundamental values we try to instill during their tender years will see them through the teen and sometimes testing years ahead, when outside allurements vie for their attention. At other times it may take intervention and some real effort on our part to help them "unlearn" a bad habit before it takes root.

When the naughty word rears its ugly head at my house, and a child is old enough to know better, I calmly sit down and explain that the word is not nice and we don't talk like that. When the word is too terrible to even attempt an explanation, I tell them just that. And then I warn, "Don't do it again," with a voice that means, "There's BIG trouble if you do." My kids *know* the tone.

With one particular child, who seemed to enjoy the shock value and response the word got from his brothers (when Mom was out of earshot), it took more than a warning or two. Sometimes a bar of soap helped get my point across.

No matter how high-tech we get with handy-wipe cleansers and neat liquid soap dispensers, for cleaning out mouths there's just nothing that can take the place of a good bar of soap. Usually it only takes one or two applications to remind children that "you are old enough to know better" and "naughty words are not spoken in our family." (I do have one child who must have enjoyed the taste. It took *several* times before he got the picture.)

You are probably aware of how pervasive vulgarity can be in movies these days. Imagine. People are paying good money to hear words that I wash my kids' mouths out for uttering.

I suppose my use of soap could be thought abusive in some circles. If kids think it's tough being kids, it's even tougher being a parent in today's world! Pornographers win awards and dine at the White House, while a militia of "parent police" stand ready to pounce on conscientious folks who dare to discipline their young.

Hey, Parents!

Watch what you say. Your child is listening and learning what is "grown-up" and acceptable—even when you think he or she isn't.

Watch what you do. Children are watching and absorbing like sponges, especially the things that are done by people they look up to and admire.

Keep your home and heart clean. There is no place for off-color, offensive or "adult" (a misnomer, to be sure) material, whether it be for reading, listening or viewing. Causing scandal or confusion for young people is serious and sinful.

Offer loving reminders. When a child is exposed to something unacceptable, this is the time to remind him or her, "We are Christians, and this kind of thing is not how we behave." Most of the time, all it takes is a word from a parent or grandparent.

> Whoever spoils his son will bind up his wounds,
> and will suffer heartache at every cry.
> An unbroken horse turns out stubborn,
> and an unchecked son turns out headstrong.
> Pamper a child, and he will terrorize you;
> play with him, and he will grieve you.
> —SIRACH 30:7–9

(I must say that there is some attraction to the thought of a day in jail with a good book, no interruptions and three square meals without spilled milk or having to cut up someone's meat. But I guess I shouldn't joke.)

The *Catechism of the Catholic Church* is clear about scandal:

> Scandal takes on a particular gravity by reason of the authority of those who cause it or the weakness of those who are scandalized. It prompted our Lord to utter this curse: "Whoever causes one of these little ones who believe in me to sin, it would be better for him to have a great millstone fastened round his neck and to be drowned in the depth of the sea" [Matthew 18:6]. (*CCC*, #2285)

The *Catechism* also reminds us,

> Blasphemy is directly opposed to the second commandment. It consists in uttering against God—inwardly or outwardly—words of hatred, reproach or defiance; in speaking ill of God; in failing in respect toward Him in one's speech; in misusing God's name.... The prohibition of blasphemy extends to language against Christ's Church, the saints and sacred things. (*CCC,* #2148)

Here the old adage is true: "Cleanliness is next to godliness!" It's really up to us parents to set the tone. We need to teach our young that they truly are temples of the Holy Spirit and that their minds, hearts and bodies should reflect God's image.

In truth, there is no place for bad language. Sometimes it may take a bar of soap as a reminder, and we might be accused of being out of touch with the times. A small price to pay! After all, our goal is not to find happiness in award-winning "entertainment" with expletives but perfect happiness for all eternity in heaven!

Christian parents discipline their children precisely because we love them. And because of this responsible love, Christian parents will continue to ignore the secular status quo and, with every fiber of their being, guide, guard and protect their young from *anything* harmful, including movies, TV, music, videos and even friendships that may rob them of their innocence and virtue. 🌴

> You are the light of the world.... Let your light shine before others so that they may see your good works and give glory to your Father in heaven.
>
> —MATTHEW 5:14, 16

16

Dealing With the Unexpected

Do not worry about tomorrow, for tomorrow will bring worries of its own. Today's trouble is enough for today.

—MATTHEW 6:34

Sometimes I feel as though my entire day is spent dealing with the unexpected. There's always another phone call, last-minute request or drop-in visitor. In fact, these surprises provide some of the greatest pleasures of life!

You could say that our son Tony was a "drop-in" surprise. He arrived from an orphanage in South Vietnam just five days after our daughter Tina arrived from the Philippines. We had four children under four and a half, three of them in diapers, so life was a bit chaotic. Yet that little "surprise," once the dust settled, was one of the greatest blessings of our young married life.

Then there are the other kinds of "unexpecteds." Like the day when I think every single second is scheduled to the max, and a kid comes down with the flu, or the school calls to tell me, "Joseph fainted in class!" Cancel all plans! Funny how our priorities shake down to what's *really* important.

In our family with thirteen children, and now with our extended family of grown children and grandchildren, we've had more than a few heart-stoppers. I remember the time Angela, then nine, collapsed in pain on the living room floor while we were in the middle of night prayers. She was rushed by ambulance to the hospital to have her appendix removed. What a night that was! Years later a similar scene was repeated with our son Dominic.

One of the scariest times for me was when my husband, John, became seriously ill and was hospitalized. How could that happen? He's not supposed to get sick.

Then there was the night our basement was flooding by the inches, destroying our boys' bedroom, playroom, storage and laundry areas. Believe me, there was *no* quick solution that would wipe away that monster problem. It was a mess!

But it's the little things in life that seem to unglue me. Like the time two of our boys tossed a ball through the living room window I was sitting in front of, with a baby on my lap, or the day we opened the mail to find the insurance company had denied coverage on a legitimate claim.

Oh, yes, big families enjoy more blessings and benefits—because of our sheer number—but we also may face more challenges!

The "lifestyle gurus" might suggest a course in "stress management" for those unsettling and unnerving situations. You know, the kind where you attend seminars and learn programmed behaviors in order to cope. We Christians know a better way. It's called *hope!*

There's nothing like an emergency to energize your prayer life, I always say!

Here's one mom who is a firm believer in spontaneous prayer, though I must confess that my initial reactions are not always prayerful. Fear seems to dominate when crisis or chaos hits. Yet no matter the worry, just whispering a prayer seems to set us on a course out of the maze and in the right direction.

And who better to plead our cause than Mary, the Mother of God? Surely she will have Christ's ear like no other. Would her Son ever ignore or refuse her prayerful pleading? *Never.*

"When Jesus saw his mother and the disciple whom he loved standing beside her, he said to his mother, 'Woman, here is your son.' Then he said to the disciple, 'Here is your mother.' And from that hour the disciple took her into his own home" (John 19:26–27).

There are many prayers I rely on when disaster strikes, whether a kid is in trouble at school, a loved one is sick or some little emergency comes up to sap my strength and stamina. I reach for the prayers that never fail to ease my mind, settle my nerves and reinforce my faith.

The rosary is one such prayer. But when it's split-second action I need, it's the Memorare I lean on. Saying this one simple prayer over and over seems to offer reassurance, calm my worst fears and help my husband and me project a calmness to our children that we may not be able to do otherwise. Hearing those words seems to set in motion my pleas for Mary's intervention in a crisis situation.

I have learned that this was a favorite prayer of Mother Teresa of Calcutta. Little wonder at what she accomplished in spite of the obstacles and opposition she encountered in her lifetime!

So if you're having one of those days or just want a beautiful prayer to whisper your love and devotion to God and his Mother, try the Memorare:

Remember, O most gracious Virgin Mary, that never was it known that anyone who fled to thy protection, implored thy help, or sought thy intercession was left unaided. Inspired with this confidence, I fly unto thee, O Virgin of virgins, my Mother. To thee do I come; before thee I stand, sinful and sorrowful. O Mother of the Word Incarnate, despise not my petitions, but in thy mercy hear and answer me. Amen.

17

Excuses, Excuses!

The man said, "The woman whom you gave to be with me—she gave me fruit from the tree, and I ate it." The LORD God then asked the woman, "What is it that you have done?" The woman answered, "The serpent tricked me, and I ate it."

—GENESIS 3:12–13

As the mother of a large family, I would venture to say that I've heard more than my fair share of excuses. "It wasn't me, I didn't do it," "Someone else must have broken it." We've been told, "That's not *my* job; it's Joe's," "Kari told me she *wanted* her hair cut that short," "I *told* Mary that you would be mad if we wore this to church, but she wouldn't listen," "Tony said that Grandma said there wasn't any poison ivy in that area," "Dominic told me the cement was dry!"

One of my favorites after a catastrophe is "Well, it wasn't *my* idea," as if that is any consolation.

Some will begrudgingly admit their guilt: "OK, I did it, but Michael did it first!"

Then there are the "No one told me" excuses: "No one told *me* not to eat that! I didn't know the cake was for your company." "No one told *me* not to touch it!" "I didn't know you were talking to me." Or a refrain often heard in a large families, "You must have told one of your other kids, but no one *ever* told *me!*"

Some children feign disappointment that we didn't recognize the inventive genius in them: "How do you think Thomas Edison ever got started?" "It was supposed to be an experiment, but it didn't work." Or this response to fungus discovered under the bed: "Oh, that! Tina was growing it for a science project at school, but then she changed her mind and forgot about it."

Sometimes the kids make us feel that it was really *our* fault: "I thought you wanted me to learn how to cook." "You were the one who told me to start making my own decisions." "How did I know you couldn't use hot water on it?" "I thought you wanted me to learn how to drive."

Of course there are the excuses that tug at your heart-strings: "Gee, I was *only* trying to help." "We were trying to surprise you and make you breakfast when Tony accidentally dropped the carton of eggs on the living room carpet." "I told Angie we should call you, but we were afraid you'd be asleep, and we didn't want to wake you!"

Then there are the innocent excuses: "I didn't know it would shrink (dissolve, fade, discolor or whatever) if it got wet." "It wasn't my fault; it *came* that way." And Charlie's classic line after starting a fire in the basement: "I didn't know the newspapers would catch on fire so quickly and spread to the paint cans!"

Sometimes the explanations can be detailed: "Oh, didn't I tell you that after we went to the dance, and after we went bowling, and after we went to Tiffany's house for the bonfire, and after we picked up a bite to eat, we were all going to hang out at Woody's for the rest of the night?"

Some have even turned religious: "I know I broke curfew when I stayed out all night, but I did go to Mass this morning before I came home." And, "Who knows? I might consider a vocation if I just had some time to myself and went to Florida (or California, Mexico…) for spring break!"

"Blame the other parent" is another tactic. One year Tim and Charlie tore up our backyard fence and put over a hundred large nails into the redwood boards. "We were just making a fort. Dad gave us the hammer and nails and told us to build something in the backyard!"

Then there are the excuses aimed at *our* compassion: "I try to get good grades and do everything you want me to do, and *one* little thing goes wrong and I'm busted. It's just not fair." Other excuses point out *their* compassion, such as the excuse Tim and Charlie offered when they tried to skip school with their friend: "Paul didn't have school, and we didn't want him to be all alone for the whole day!"

If I had more time and more paper, I'm sure I could catalogue a few more of the excuses we've heard as parents through the years. But then I get to thinking of our Father in heaven and all the flimsy excuses for wrongdoing he hears from *us* every day! We're as good as our first parents at shifting the blame.

What is so wonderful about our faith is knowing that we have a Father in heaven who loves us unconditionally and wants to forgive our sins and failings. In fact, he will give us everything we need to help us be happy for all eternity. And all we need do is ask him! There's really no excuse for failure, then, is there?

> Rejoice in hope, be patient in suffering, persevere in prayer.
>
> —ROMANS 12:12

18

A Retreat for the Teens in Your Life

Grow in the grace and knowledge of our Lord and
Savior Jesus Christ.

—2 PETER 3:18

One of our family rules—and though my kids might
tell you differently, there aren't that many—is that each of
our children must make a weekend retreat before graduating from high school. Is it a rule they like? No. But it's one
we have not backed down from, no matter the whining or
good excuses. And believe me, we've heard just about
everything.

Some of our older children tried telling us, "I'm too
busy," or, "I can't take time off work." (We assured them
that their gas station and donut shop jobs would be there
when they returned.) One son told us, "You're just wasting
your money. I'm already Catholic!" Another objected that
the daylong retreat at his Catholic high school was about
"all he could handle." He went anyway. Funny what you
can handle when you have to.

Our most recent candidate was Michael, then sixteen
and a junior in high school. He fussed a bit but offered no
real resistance to the retreat rule. One of the benefits of
having a large family is that by the time a rule hits the
younger ones, they've learned that it's not debatable. No
one else wriggled out of it, so there's no use trying.

I told Michael, "It won't kill you. In fact, you might like it so much that you'll want to sign up for more."

"Actually," he said, "I'm going to make out my last will before I go. I plan to leave my CDs to Dominic, just in case I don't come back."

Something spiritually powerful occurs in the mere process of removing sons and daughters from the pressures and pleasures that confront *every* teen and young adult in today's world. A retreat offers them the gift of time: time to think, to ponder, to imagine and to reason about where they are going and what is their ultimate goal—heaven, we hope!

Unfortunately there are millions, young and old, who wander through life never really knowing their purpose or the loving God who awaits them. John and I want much more for our children than what secular society sells as "success" or happiness. God promises much more! And what better tool to help us tell them that than a retreat with others who share that heavenly vision?

Some Good Retreats

For teens and young adults:

- TEC (Teens Encounter Christ)
- NET (National Evangelization Team)

For adults:

- Engaged Encounter
- Marriage Encounter
- Cursillo Movement
- Silent retreats, directed and nondirected

To find out about retreats in your area, call your local diocese.

There are many fine retreat opportunities for teens and young adults. The TEC (Teens Encounter Christ) experience is the one most familiar to our family. Although it is open to people of all ages, TEC seems purposely designed with young people in mind. Not one from our batch has returned disappointed! The weekend is built around the sacraments of reconciliation and the Eucharist. The uplifting activities throughout the three days not only hold their attention and heighten their participation but also prompt many to return later for scheduled "reunions."

Our daughter Mary concedes that the experience may not work for everyone, but it's been a wonderful and rewarding time for her. "The secret to making a good retreat," she says, "is to be *open*. It won't work for people who have made up their minds they're not going to like it."

Yet even for some of ours who initially felt "forced" to go, the end result was positive. For a few the experience was life changing!

During her college years our daughter Kari saw TEC as such a positive in her life that she spent many weekends volunteering. Eventually she became a staff member and coordinator, something she never dreamed would happen when she attended her first retreat weekend.

"I grew up in a Catholic family," Kari bubbled enthusiastically, "but at TEC I realized for the first time that I needed to choose this for myself and to try to live it out in my everyday life."

Her experiences echo those of her older siblings. The wonderful results these retreats have brought about in our children are a welcome reinforcement of our Catholic beliefs. In fact, over the years five of our daughters and sons returned to work as volunteers on other retreats.

As for Michael, did he survive? Yes, he returned home to reclaim his CDs from Dominic. And his impression of the retreat? "It was awesome, *really* awesome," he said.

"I have to admit, the first day wasn't easy," he confided. "I thought to myself, 'What am I doing here? I want to leave.' But it got better and better. I really had no idea it was going to be that good!"

TEC didn't end there for Michael either. "I'm going to work on a couple of my buddies," he said. "I think they'd really like it if they gave it a chance!" Now, that's an endorsement!

Some family rules are worth fighting for. 🌳

> Strive first for the kingdom of God and his righteousness, and all these things will be given to you as well.
> —MATTHEW 6:33

19

Weight Lifting Your Way to Heaven?

My sons Michael (twenty) and Joseph (sixteen) are into weight lifting—big time. Both play football—Michael for college and Joseph for high school—that is, when they're not on the bench nursing their injuries. Never mind the bruises, breaks and sprains that have occasionally kept them off the field and on the sofa, far more than they'd like to talk about. They *love* the game and say it's well worth the pain.

What part of this am I supposed to understand?

Weight lifting has now become part of the boys' daily regimen. Michael brought home some used equipment he picked up from a buddy who either moved onto "bigger" things or is now so "buffed" (I think that's the lingo they use) he has no further need of it. At any rate, the boys are certain they "got a deal," and that this equipment will improve their athletic ability.

Walking into Michael and Joseph's room, since the introduction of weight lifting, is like strolling through an obstacle course. (I don't go in there too often, only once in a while to see where my laundry baskets have disappeared to—usually near Michael's bed, heaped with his unfolded clothes.) The weight equipment nestles in among their already abundant collection of bats, balls, darts and dart-boards, pucks and hockey sticks, gloves, caps, masks, hel-mets and hoops. I maneuver around barbells, long metal poles, an enormous stack of iron disks—the size of one is comparable to that of a large pizza and is too heavy to even budge—and an eight-foot weight bench!

All this in a room that's supposed to be for rest. And to think three of my girls once occupied this room, and I dared complain about the messiness of Barbie dolls and hairbrushes lying around! Oh, for the days!

Have you noticed that boys never seem to be both-ered by dust and disarray? In their eyes the room looks cozy and "lived in." Every so often I get upset with the clutter and threaten them with a $15 fine (good lunch money for a girlfriend and me). Then they hustle to put things in order.

My husband has figured out how to use the boys' bodybuilding zeal to his advantage. He'll catch Joseph as he comes in the back door after school. "Joseph," he says, "I've got some weight lifting for you!"

"OK, Dad," Joseph says.

"There's an old car battery on the garage floor. I want you to carry it in and put it on the work bench in the base-ment," John explains.

And off Joseph goes to the garage.

Where have I failed? Why can't I think of some clever incentive to get the Mr. Americas in my family to think that carrying out the overflowing trash or taking the recyclables to the garage is an invaluable part of their weight-lifting regimen? No, they just walk around it all without a back-ward glance. Why can't an overflowing trash bin have some of the appeal of a stacked barbell?

My boys are convinced that "building muscle tone" is not only important for their own sports activity but also would benefit everyone else's physical health. In fact, Joseph recently chose the topic of weight lifting for a class research and speech project. He probably chose this topic to counter some of his mother's objections to "too much time being spent lifting dumbbells." He told his class that "my mom is critical of weight lifting" and "thinks I'll get muscle-bound if I do too much."

Wait a minute! I never worried about his getting "muscle-bound" lifting the trash, pushing the vacuum or lawnmower or doing too many chores around the house.

Joseph's research was thought-provoking and thorough. He told the class, "You might be thinking that only old people need to worry about their bones, but experts say that the critical years for building bone mass are pre-adolescence to age thirty. Weight lifting also helps prevent and rehabilitate injuries due to thinner bones and increases flexibility and strength. For example, if you have been injured, your doctor may advise you to lift weights or perform certain exercises during the healing process."

He even gently pointed out to me the advantages of exercise and weight lifting for "older women." (Hmmmm!) They help build bone density and combat the onset of osteoporosis.

Joseph is right in his concern about our bodies and our health. We always want to take good care of what God has generously given to us. But I believe that it is my responsibility to watch over my children and to remind them that too much of *anything*—especially when it has to do with "perfecting" our bodies—can be a distraction and temptation. Whether it's beauty, brains or brawn, the rule is "All things in moderation."

I want all my sons and daughters to know that beauty and muscle are fleeting. What really counts is knowing to whom we belong and where we are going. We must never forget that our number-one goal is not good looks or wealth, but heaven. And when things in life get us down, as they sometimes do, Jesus will always be there to lift the weight of our burden. All we need do is turn to him and ask. 🌲

> Come to me, all you that are weary and are carrying heavy burdens, and I will give you rest.
>
> —MATTHEW 11:28

20

Gen and Lu

Gen and her husband Lu were like family to us. They lived up the street and were members of our church, where Lu (at ninety-two) still serves faithfully each Sunday as an usher.

Gen and Lu delighted in seeing our brood pour into the front pews each week (we needed two for many years). Often they would stop to chat with us after Mass, taking an interest in each child, asking how he or she was doing in school, sports and life in general.

They were a special couple indeed. Married sixty-three years, Gen and Lu were active in church, clubs and community. They had no children of their own, so they doted on their godchildren, nieces and nephews, as well as the other children in their lives—like the Kuharskis down the block.

We were an expensive family to take a liking to. I don't think there was a school marathon, band fundraiser or other sponsored event for which they didn't support the Kuharski kids over the years—and always with the generosity that hallmarks "the cheerful giver."

But the greatest gift Gen and Lu gave to my kids didn't come in sponsorships or providing yard and snow jobs. Their gift was intangible and far greater.

It began when Gen lost her ability to speak. In the beginning she still came to church each week, dressed in her "Sunday best" browns, peach or pastels, always with matching purse and hat. No longer able to communicate verbally, she would stand at Lu's side as he chatted and teased our children, nodding and smiling as if to say, "Ditto for me!"

Gradually Gen's health deteriorated, and she was no longer able to attend church. Soon she was bedridden and totally dependent upon Lu for feeding, dressing and all of her personal care needs. But a nursing home was out of the question. "She's my sweetheart," Lu would say. "She'll do best at home with me."

And so Lu learned to skillfully care for Gen's daily medical needs. And for those occasions when he had to be away, he compiled a list of trusted helpers he could call on to sit with Gen.

Our Michael, Kari, Dominic, Angie, Mary and Joseph were privileged to be part of Lu's team of helpers, watching Gen so that Lu could get to church and usher on Sundays, shop for groceries, visit a friend or sing with the Knights of Columbus men's choir, one of his favorite activities.

Lu always made sure our youngsters were generously compensated for their time. He wouldn't have it any other way.

In their first fifty-three years of marriage, Gen had been the homemaker and "doer," looking after Lu's needs. She was his helpmate and companion, even traveling with him when he was on long business assignments. Now *he* was the companion and comforter.

Gen's disease was debilitating, and the "dying process," as they say, took not days or weeks but years.

Yet Lu never wavered in his quiet determination and his devotion to Gen.

What really struck our children was that no matter the prognosis or the obvious decline in Gen's health, Lu remained cheerful and at peace in his daily caregiving. On each visit our kids would see this kind and gentle man bending lovingly over his wife, who lay motionless in her at-home hospital bed, unable to respond or react. He would pat her reassuringly, kiss her sweetly on her hands and face and say, "I won't be long now, Sweetheart. You be good for Michael here, and I'll be back soon."

Lu liked to reminisce about when they first met. It was a sweetheart story every one of our family enjoyed hearing.

"You should have seen how pretty she was the first time I saw her in the lunchroom at Edison High School," he would boast. "I thought to myself, 'Wow! She's pretty!' And you know what? She's the *only* girlfriend I ever had!"

"What a contrast," Kari (then eighteen) confided one day. "Today's world tells us to have as many partners as possible. But look at Mr. V. He's always so cheerful. And he's so happy being faithful to his one and only love!"

"In sickness and in health, until death us do part."

As time passed, our children became more than spectators and neighbors. Their affection grew for both Lu and Gen, along with their admiration. Sometimes they would return home, after an evening with Gen, full of conversation. At other times they would say little more than, "It's just so sad. But he's so good to her." There were times too when their tears would well over the situation.

After a ten-year illness, God in his mercy called Gen home. Though she spoke not a word in those ten years, she and her faithful husband Lu taught my children a great lesson in the profound mystery of married love. "Husbands, love your wives, just as Christ loved the church and gave himself up for her" (Ephesians 5:25).

The story of Gen and Lu offers some valuable lessons to all of us:

- The best lesson in love is not taught but caught. Kids learn by osmosis. Have them hang around those who are happily living out their sacramental union. What better teacher to counteract a culture of "divorce for *any* reason or no reason at all" than to let our children witness couples who are loving and faithful.

- No one has a perfect, pain-free, carefree life. We live in an imperfect world and sad things happen. But God promises all the grace necessary for whatever difficulties come our way. All we need do is ask. Point out to your children people who are living the way God calls them to live in spite of the obstacles they face.

- Take your children to visit those you know who are elderly, shut-in or sick (if appropriate). The simplicity and joy of children is one of the most contagious cures for sickness and loneliness.

- Watch for the miracles when you and your young take time to visit someone who is ailing or alone. It is a corporal work of mercy, and God's graces flow when you see Jesus and offer comfort to those who appear, as Mother Teresa often said, "in distressing disguise."

- Attend wakes and funerals with your children. They may not fully understand (nor may we) the passing from this life to eternal life, but we can help them realize that while we are sad to lose a loved one, we can rejoice because God promises a special place for those who are faithful to him. 🌲

He will wipe every tear from their eyes.
Death will be no more;
mourning and crying and pain will be no more,
for the first things have passed away.

—REVELATION 21:4

21

Do I Get a Trophy?

Have you ever had the sinking feeling that you just don't fit in? It happened to me one evening when I attended my son Michael's high school football banquet.

Everyone, the kids as well as the parents, couldn't have been nicer or more welcoming. Nevertheless, it didn't take long for me to know that I was, pardon the expression, "out of my league."

My first inkling came, innocently enough, when the parents at our table started swapping stories of some of the year's most memorable games. Realizing that I couldn't tell the difference between a halfback (which sounds as if part of his torso is missing) and a fullback, I sat in silence. But then a sweet mom sitting two chairs down from me leaned over and said, "Your Michael is such a *good* player."

"Oh, is he?" I responded before I could catch myself. "Thank you," I smiled (as if I had anything to do with it).

Unfortunately, I couldn't return the compliment about her son, because I had absolutely no clue as to whether he was a player, record-keeper, cheerleader or water boy. (He was one of the star players, I later learned.) In truth I couldn't recall if my own son played offense or defense on the field. I thought it was nice that I remembered their colors were blue and white. (I like pretty uniforms.)

I leaned over when no one was looking and asked my husband in a soft whisper, "What does Michael play?" Tight end, I learned. That's a position? Hmmmm.

Actually, I had attended only portions of three of Michael's games that season, which was two more than I had attended for his younger brother Joseph. My recollection of football is not of the games or plays but of the broken or swollen limbs, stitches, bandages and ice packs that make me continually ask, "I thought this was supposed to be a sport. Why does it have to be so rough?"

In one season alone Joseph suffered a broken leg and Michael needed twenty stitches in his arm and pulled a tendon in his leg. Never mind the emergency room or doctor visits, not to mention the pain: Both boys couldn't wait until next season.

Back to the banquet. After our catered buffet, the coaches (I learned there is more than one) each gave a speech, describing in nearly perfect play-by-play recollection the highlights of the season. I sat mesmerized as my eyes began to glaze over. How do they remember with such accuracy the minutes and seconds, not to mention the plays and players, of something that happened weeks ago?

But the real highlight of the evening was the presentation of the trophies and awards to the players.

The first player to accept his trophy sauntered to the microphone and began his acceptance speech with "I'd like to thank our coaches and especially my parents, who attended *all* my games...."

I began to wonder if this was being televised.

The second honored player offered a similar refrain: "I want to thank my parents, who were 'there for me' [I love that phrase] and *never* missed one of my games...." And so too the third.

Michael, who was sitting a table away, looked over at me, and we both began to roll our eyes and chuckle. "I wonder if Michael will get a special award for having a mother who does NOT attend his games," I whispered to John, who loves attending our kids' sports events.

"I'm sure with your size family, it's hard for you to make all of the games," more than one consoling parent has offered in my defense. Yes, and a few years ago, when we had six teens at once and children involved in piano, band, track, cross-country, basketball, soccer, volleyball, softball, football and high school golf, it would have been quite a feat! It would be a good escape to feign that I'd be in the front row belting out my kid's name if I only had one or two to dote over. But it wouldn't be the truth.

Now, I believe in the value of having children play some kind of sport (if possible), as well as a musical instrument. These help them to be well-rounded. They not only benefit from learning a skill but also from the discipline and practice.

Children need to play, to learn how to do their best and hopefully to enjoy an occasional win. Team building and getting along with others are valuable lessons that will stay with them throughout life. And there is a valuable lesson in losing that involves congratulating opponents and accepting defeat; it's called good sportsmanship.

So why don't I attend all the games to cheer my youngsters on? Because I don't believe it's necessary. In fact, I don't think it is healthy or helpful.

Kids should be free from undue pressure and know that it's not the end of the world if they fumble, fall or foul out. But when parents interrupt their working schedules to attend an event, it becomes more than a game, and the kids know it. Recreation and enjoyment may still be important, but now there is more riding on the game—namely, pleasing adults, especially Mom and Dad.

It goes without saying that most parents are the best of folks who enjoy attending and desire nothing more than a "good game" for their young. But we must remember what children's sports are supposed to be. I know of more than one dad who recorded *every* game on his camcorder and then played it for his son at home so they could "perfect his play." And some kids barely make it off the field or court before the parent is asking, "What happened to you?"

Sadder still, I've seen some adults lose control at children's events, screaming, cursing and taunting coaches and players when a game didn't go their way. I've seen time-outs called for disruptive and unruly behavior—not from the kids but from the parents in the stands. Some, in fact, were banned from future games. Good sportsmanship? Hardly, and the example is not lost, even on distracted Little Leaguers.

Most of us played sports as youngsters. Sometimes it was little more than a gathering of neighborhood kids in a vacant sandlot. But even in the organized competitive sports, our folks rarely if ever attended. They were busy providing for us, and somehow we never felt slighted or deprived. We knew we were number one in their lives—whether we lost or won—and that they were doing the best they could to prepare us for the only prize that really matters: heaven.

That's what I want for my children, and I don't have to know the difference between a halfback and a fullback to get them there! Thank heavens! 🌲

> I press on toward the goal for the prize of the heavenly call of God in Christ Jesus.
> —PHILIPPIANS 3:14

22

Parents Can Come in Handy

Did you ever "blame it on your parents" when you were a kid? Well, I did, and it got me off the hook and out of some pretty tight spots on more than one occasion. If I was being urged to go someplace or do something that I *knew* was trouble, I'd beg off with "I can't go. I asked my mom, and I'll be grounded *forever* if I don't get right home!"

That was the end of it. The pressure was off. It made my folks and their rules look like the "bad guys," and I saved face. Those were the times I was grateful for my parents' "archaic" rules and curfews. Of course, I never told them.

Now that I'm the mom, I've given my kids blanket permission to "blame it on me" when a sticky situation arises and they need a good excuse. Tony, who seemed to collect trouble for a hobby when he was a teen, once confided, "I told my buddies, 'My mom is Italian, and I tell ya, you don't want to mess with her. It's not worth it!'" He oughta know.

We must remember that our goal for our children is far different from that of their peers and perhaps even adult mentors. We're so nuts about our young, we want their happiness not just now but *forever* in heaven. That's why we're willing to risk being unpopular in order to keep them "on track" and away from temptation and trouble.

Kids *need* parents, even when they're sure they don't. That's why they are children and we are the parents. They are far more comfortable and confident when they know the rules. It offers them a sense of security and a rhythm to everyday life that is unchanging and unyielding. Heaven knows they have enough confusing signals coming at them from the outside, the secular world, which cares little about their body or soul.

I think children need and want limits. They want to know where they stand and what is expected of them. Isn't that as God intends? Christ's obedience to Mary and Joseph at the finding in the temple is our best example: "Then he went down with them and came to Nazareth, and was obedient to them" (Luke 2:51).

The ability to make sound decisions comes with maturity. Even simple choices for a young child can appear weighty. For instance, have you ever asked one to choose what to have for dinner or dessert or what to wear? The answer, preceded by, "Ummmm," seems to take forever. Younger children sense security when parents make basic decisions for them.

Let's face it, no matter how disciplined and bright a child may be, there's no match for an adult's experience and maturity. Grown-ups offer a healthy perception and perhaps distance in confronting situations. They are far more likely to consider the *long-range* effects before acting.

Children, on the other hand, have that wonderful quality of spontaneity. They are impetuous, impulsive and loaded with curiosity. The same quality that urges them to shovel the walk for an elderly neighbor or come to the rescue of a child being bullied is the one that will look you square in the eye when asked, "Didn't you stop and *think* before you did it?" and will innocently respond, "No." They mean it. They just didn't think.

A study published by the Insurance Institute for Highway Safety bears this out. The report revealed that motor vehicle crashes are the number one killer of teens. The causes are not alcohol or drug abuse, as some may think, but rather speeding, failure to stay in a lane and being distracted while driving. In other words, kids just do not *think* of the consequences. That's called *poor judgment*.[1]

OK, so I happen to be one of those "old-fashioned" folks who believe that children really do need the guidance and counsel of loving parents, even when they insist they are old enough to make their own decisions. I'm sure there is a host of professionals and parents who have a different philosophy, but this is one mom who rules with tight reins. Just ask any of my thirteen kids, some of whom have told their friends, "My mom doesn't live in this century."

My daughter Kari once called home from college and remarked, "My roommates think you're so cute, Mom. But I told them, 'She's cute, all right. Try living with her!'"

Do we "loosen the reins" as they grow? Absolutely. Yet we must never assume that teens and young adults don't need or won't benefit from our insight, discernment and direction. Translated, that means, "We love you so much that we are setting down household rules that we believe are best for your well-being and ours."

Yes, there have been times when we've set curfews for *our* benefit. We don't want our "castle" invaded in the middle of the night by young adults who enjoy living in a different time zone!

There are those today who suggest that when it comes to teens and young adults, "too much supervision" (whatever that means) is unnecessary and overprotective. But our son Tony gave us, without realizing it, a good tip when he confided, "My friend Bob told me, 'You mean you still have a curfew at nineteen? Well, I guess I think you're pretty lucky at that. At least you know your folks care. My parents told me I was old enough to set my *own* limits.'"

Kuharskis, don't even think about it! 🌳

23

What About Manners and Modesty?

Shun youthful passions and pursue righteousness, faith, love, and peace, along with those who call on the Lord from a pure heart.

—2 TIMOTHY 2:22

If I want to start a real one-way conversation at our house or watch my kids' eyes roll, all I have to do is say, "Well, when I was young we had to…," or, "Look at that! What ever happened to manners and modesty?"

"I didn't think *anyone* talked about manners and modesty anymore," a waitress blurted out after overhearing my remarks. Well, this mom does!

Caps and sweatbands, scruffy T-shirts and weathered jeans used to be saved for baling hay, greasing cars or painting the house. Today they're part of the "casual" look, seen in even the most refined places.

My pet peeve is baseball caps pasted atop otherwise handsome heads. Has no one bothered to tell them, even *insist*, that removing a cap is the mannerly thing to do when you're in a home, dining out, attending church or "in the presence of a lady"?

My boys don't appreciate my "hats off" rule, but it comes with the parenting package. We've even shared our wisdom with some of their friends: "I know, Mrs. K., 'Hats off in the house, '"' they say as they come through our back door. Neat guys!

I was the *only* mother with such archaic notions, my kids thought, until one day on vacation we walked into a restaurant to eat and our son quietly removed his cap. A man in a nearby booth walked over to Michael and said, "I knew immediately that you were from a well-mannered family when I saw you remove your hat at the dinner table. Keep it up, boy. You've got good parents!"

That man must have been my guardian angel in disguise.

Pardon me if my age is showing, but what has happened to "dressing up" rather than "dressing down"? Is there some prize given to the one who can look the grungiest? Will the guy in the ad with the "five o'clock shadow" soon sport a toothless grin or a mouthful of decayed teeth?

Sound crazy? Take a peek at a fashion magazine, *any* fashion magazine, and you'll see countless models with blackened eyes and bony bodies. It's called the "heroin" or "cocaine" look, and it's *chic!*

Worse, the filthy language and crude conduct once confined to the unwashed, uneducated and unrefined is now routinely accepted as *vogue* in some circles. Even women use it.

Something more than clothes and conduct is at stake here. The very soul of our society seems bent on the purposeful promotion of all that is indecent, immodest and impure.

The blame in part goes to the celebrities and sports heroes whose boorish behavior continually insults our integrity and assaults the innocence of our youth. We see it *everywhere:* in ads, at the movies, at the beach, on the streets— and in our home if we permit it. And that's the point.

"Where are their parents?" my kids hear me murmur. Does no one love them enough to tell them—no, insist for their own good—about manners and modesty?

Boys need to know that the *real* man isn't the guy who gives in to every whim and sexual urge but the one who shows willpower, self-control, chastity and consideration for the needs and welfare of others, especially vulnerable young women.

Girls need to understand that what they wear, or don't wear, may be a source of temptation to young men, an occasion of serious sin. A *real* lady takes care to wear clothing that won't cause scandal or shame or call into question her intentions or good reputation. In other words, scanty bikinis, low-cut dresses and other revealing outfits are out!

"God did not call us to impurity but in holiness. Therefore whoever rejects this rejects not human authority but God, who also gives his Holy Spirit to you" (1 Thessalonians 4:7–8).

Manners show our respect for other people. Modesty shows our reverence for God's laws, our own bodies and the bodies of others.

Parents make a big mistake when they *assume* their children know about manners and modesty. They don't unless we tell them, and occasionally remind them again.

Here are some morsels on modesty and morals we've passed on to our youngsters:

✐ Watch your language. Foul or suggestive language labels you and can ruin your reputation. If in doubt, decide if you can say the same thing in front of your mother or grandmother. If not, don't say it. Remember, once spoken, words can't be taken back.

◈ Especially show respect for God and the things of God. Remember the second commandment, "You shall not make wrongful use of the name of the LORD your God, for the LORD will not acquit anyone who misuses his name" (Exodus 20:7).

◈ Watch your behavior. There is no room for behaving immorally and consuming illicit drink or drugs if you want others to respect you and to know you as a person of integrity.

◈ What you wear tells others *who* you are. A person of good moral character won't wear clothing that's immodest. You are a child of God, and your body is a temple of the Holy Spirit. Being clean and carefully clothed lets others see and think the best of you!

◈ Watch your manners. Anyone can behave like a slob. The person who is remembered is the one who demonstrates courtesy, consideration and kindness toward others, even in the smallest ways, such as shaking hands, holding doors open and offering help to others.

◈ Exercise willpower and self-control. Resist the wrong and do the right, even if it means you're going against the pressure of peers. It takes real courage to stand out in a crowd and do what's right. When you do, you will *never* have regrets.

◈ Build your body and your soul. The old adage is true, "Idle minds are the devil's tools!" So keep busy. Stay away from the people and things that will tempt you. Go to confession frequently. The sacrament of reconciliation offers forgiveness when you fail, and its powerful grace will renew your spiritual strength and self-control.

✐ Remember that you're part of a family. How you look, talk and behave is a reflection on your family and their standards. Show everyone your best!

✐ Rely on God's grace. God promises to supply all the grace needed to resist temptation. All you need to do is ask. Pray daily that God will guide you and protect you from temptation and danger.

✐ Take your guardian angel and the Blessed Mother along. Ask them to pray for your protection from both spiritual and physical danger. They will!

✐ Be a real leader. You are a child of God, made in his image. Our faith calls us to live differently and to offer this hope to others. You can be a living witness to those who have no such faith or standards. Be a real friend to someone who may have no one else in his or her life to turn to or look up to. ❧

The grace of God has appeared, bringing salvation to all, training us to renounce impiety and worldly passions, and in the present age to live lives that are self-controlled, upright, and godly, while we wait for the blessed hope and the manifestation of the glory of our great God and Savior, Jesus Christ.

—TITUS 2:11–13

24

Wedding Plans

I don't think there is anything more exciting for an entire family than a wedding. Not just the immediate family but grandmas, grandpas, aunts, uncles, cousins and friends from near and far come together to celebrate the occasion. What could be better?

Little wonder then that Christ chose just such an occasion to begin his public ministry: "Jesus did this, the first of his signs, in Cana of Galilee, and revealed his glory; and his disciples believed in him" (John 2:11).

When our daughter Chrissy married Andy, John opened his pocketbook and covered his eyes. When a couple prepares for and enters into marriage as God intended, no price tag can measure the joy and excitement, not to mention the blessings that come to the bride and groom and the entire family. Not that we don't watch what we spend. We compare prices, bargain shop and cut corners wherever possible. But in the end, a wedding day is a day to celebrate!

Six years later we celebrated our son Tim's wedding to Tina. And not long ago two of our daughters, Mary Elizabeth and Angela, married within eleven months of each other.

When Mary Elizabeth met Tim, her Prince Charming, we could see from the beginning that there was something special about this young man. I'd never seen her so happy, and we loved him too! Tim is the kind of guy who actually enjoys our family get-togethers. He has never been caught holding his hands over his ears to control the noise level or begging to leave early because of a "headache." He fits!

The frosting on the cake for us was the night Tim called John and me to ask if he could come over to "talk with us." Mary was out of town for her work and did not know about his visit. Tim planned to surprise her with a proposal and a ring, but *first* he wanted to ask for our blessing! Is this the twenty-first century?

Tim not only asked our permission but also showed us the ring he had selected, with the help of Mary's younger sister, Angie, who seemed to know just what Mary would like. By the time Mary returned from her business trip the next evening, everyone but she knew about the engagement, including the entire Kuharski crew, close family and friends, the people on John's E-mail list and the guys he had golfed with that morning!

Mary didn't mind one bit. After the big announcement the parents got together and a date was set.

Our anticipation heightened as arrangements were made for the reception, invitations, flowers, photographer and all the rest. And of course we women took time for what we like best: *shopping* for dresses!

I must admit that it had been a few years since I had shopped for wedding attire, and I was ill prepared for what is now considered *fashionable*. Mary took me along the first time, but I think she and her sisters wished they'd left me at home when I saw what is now considered appropriate dress for a bride and bridesmaids. Collars and cuffs are out. Backless and strapless are in!

"What is this? Where's the top?" I asked one clerk. "Maybe some girls are getting married at the Follies Review in Vegas, but we need something for CHURCH!"

It was a challenge, to be sure, but Mary found a lovely dress, and her sister Chrissy did all the alterations. Mary walked down the aisle on her father's arm in something that was both beautiful and appropriate for such a sacred occasion.

And that's the point. So many in today's culture are totally unaware of what matrimony *really* is. All we need to do is pick up the paper or the latest magazine to read of the celebrities who openly flaunt their affairs and serial ceremonies, not to mention the couples who live together first "to see if they're compatible" and those who make "prenuptial contracts" regarding children, property and unfaithfulness. The concept of sacred and "till death do us part" commitment seems all but lost in the crassness and frivolity. Little wonder that so many marriages end up in trouble or divorce.

Christian marriage is built on something far more solid though intangible: faith and God's gift of grace, which come to each couple who solemnly join together in sacramental union with Christ. Let's face it. Christians live differently than nonbelievers; we really are a counterculture. This is obvious in the care we take in preparing for marriage. A wedding is more than a party or extended prom event. Christian marriage is a sacred covenant involving a trinity of three: husband, wife and God himself.

"For this reason a man will leave his father and mother and be joined to his wife, and the two will become one flesh" (Ephesians 5:31).

Pope John Paul II often referred to husbands and wives as the "domestic church," because it is within the family that faith and the love of God are first experienced, shared and nurtured with children, the "fruit" of married love.[1] We know who does *not* want to build a domestic church for Christ but rather chaos, infidelity and sin: Satan himself! His plan is to denigrate the sacredness of marriage as well as the children who come from its union.

Pope John Paul II wrote:

> The family is placed at the center of the great struggle between good and evil, between life and death, between love and all that is opposed to love. To the family is entrusted the task of striving, first and foremost to unleash the forces of good, the source of which is found in Christ, the redeemer of man. Every family unit needs to make these forces their own so that…the family will be "strong with the strength of God."[2]

No wonder this pope wrote an entire apostolic exhortation to encourage families in our sacramental roles. In it he stated, "The future of humanity passes by way of the family."[3]

The *Catechism* says,

> Marriage is not a purely human institution…. Since God created him man and woman, their mutual love becomes an image of the absolute and unfailing love with which God loves man. It is good, very good, in the Creator's eyes. And this love which God blesses is intended to be fruitful and to be realized in the common work of watching over creation: "And God blessed them, and God said to them: 'Be fruitful and multiply, and fill the earth and subdue it'" (*CCC*, #1603, 1604).

Catholic couples are indeed blessed with a rich spiritual tradition, which promises that we are not alone as we take our wedding vows at the altar. We have an entire faith community who prays for us as we join together in sacred union. Best of all, God's grace will be there "for richer, for poorer, in sickness and in health, till death do us part."

And *that* is worth celebrating! 🌲

25

How Many Priests Can We Fit at the Dinner Table?

So, how many priests were at the dinner table this Easter?" Tony recently asked when he called home. It's not an unusual question in our family, because the kids know that if there is an opportunity to invite a seminarian or priest over, I will.

It doesn't hurt that we live just down the street from the church. Often the priests and the visiting seminarians walk or jog right past our kitchen window.

"I think Father Johnson walks extra slow when he gets to our house, just knowing you'll invite him in if you see him," Kari says.

Father Johnson teases back, "I only come to make sure Kari has enough dishes to wash" (not her favorite chore).

There's no denying that this family has a special place in our hearts for priests. Let's face it, anyone who can survive a meal with fifteen hungry Kuharskis deserves a special place!

I realized that our kids had an unrealistic impression of the priesthood when our son Charlie (then six) asked after Mass one Sunday, "Does the priest ever get to leave the church? I sure wouldn't want to be a priest. They must not have *any* fun."

If we ever wanted to promote the priesthood in our family, *that* impression would have to change. And so we resolved to get to know some priests. And what better way than at the dinner table?

It mattered little to them if our home was picture-perfect or the entrée was gourmet. Our guests were delighted to be invited and were great company! We soon became accustomed to having seminarians and priests over for an evening with the family, playing board games or cards, shooting "hoops" in the backyard or sharing laughs over an old movie from my vintage collection. And when sickness or trouble has come along, as it inevitably has, we've known the consolation and prayers of those same priests.

Father Mark Dosh has been a close family friend since he knocked on my front door and offered a personal donation for the pro-life work I was doing. He sat at my kitchen table talking politics and issues, almost oblivious to the children and "creative" chaos around us. Growing up the youngest of six, Father said he was at home with the noise and interruptions.

Father Dosh is known in more scholarly circles as a former seminary philosophy professor and bioethics consultant on medical and moral issues. But to the Kuharskis he is known and loved for his wonderful wit and competitive spirit, especially when it comes to board games and cards.

"Father Dosh always hums one of his tunes as we're playing a game, and we always suspect he has a good move coming up when his humming gets louder," Chrissy said. "We're on to him!"

Father Mark Huberty came to our church as a newly ordained priest. Our kids and the parish youth group will always remember him as the priest who took them camping, skiing and sailing. He taught them how to maneuver a tipped boat in the rushing waters of the Boundary Waters Canoe Area. He later devoted a sermon to the humility, patience and other "learning experiences" that came about while camping with a bunch of high-spirited teens.

One summer our family took Father Huberty water skiing at Grandma K's cabin. He ended up rushing to the emergency room with a punctured eardrum as a result of a bad spill.

"That was another sermon," Kari chimed. "He's gotten plenty of material for his homilies from his experiences with *our* family, even though he doesn't mention us by name." The kids love him!

Father Tollefson, our new associate pastor, knows just how to mix a guitar with religious music to keep teens' attention and interest. A convert to the faith during his college days, his talks on Catholicism and the priesthood are vibrant and inspiring. Our sons Michael, Dominic and Joseph are even more impressed by Father's openness.

"He's really not afraid to try new situations," Joseph said. "Father learned how to downhill ski right along with us when we went on the youth group trip. It was pretty fun."

This mom was just thankful they *all* returned with no broken bones or stitches!

Father Johnson, now working toward his doctorate in Rome, was assigned for six months to our parish as a young seminarian. Each week he would show up at the seventh- and eighth-grade boys' baseball and basketball games, loaded with pop and treats for the kids. Talk about making a favorable impression!

There isn't a kid in our school who doesn't know that Father Johnson loves being a priest. He delights in saying to the boys, "Hey, you'd look great in black! You should think seriously about being a priest!"

Our children grew up with Father Francis Kittock as our pastor. For twenty-seven years he led our edge-of-the-city parish through the ups and downs of the demographic changes that have affected most major cities. His managerial approach and "no nonsense" style led some to suggest he was stern, "aloof" or unapproachable. But to the grade school children at St. Charles's, Father Kittock was a role model. Children were "top priority" to Father, and he made sure they knew it!

When it came time for graduation, Father would take each eighth grader aside for "a little talk." In his "fatherly" style he would ask each what his or her plans were for high school and beyond. Then he would say, "Don't forget, St. Charles is your home parish. You are always welcome here. I'll be watching for you and praying for you."

Father Kittock has never played cards with our children or taken them camping, but whenever they had a question regarding faith or morals, they would not hesitate to call him. In fact, one of our sons, while serving in the military, would call Father Kittock long-distance when he was stumped by anti-Catholic arguments.

"Father Kittock is such a father figure to me," our daughter Angie said. "He's authoritative but always gentle and caring. That's why I always used to jump in his line for confession!"

In addition to seminarians and priests, we've met a few bishops over the years. Our kids met Bishop Paul Dudley, former bishop of Sioux Falls, South Dakota, after a Saturday evening Mass. "We're all going out to my favorite place to eat tonight," Bishop Dudley declared. "Yup, it's where I take all the visiting dignitaries, and it's MY treat: McDonalds!"

The kids were delighted! As we walked through the fast-food chain that evening, balancing our trays heaped with burgers and fries, we could hear Bishop Dudley teasing the teens who worked behind the counter. "Hey, our basketball team is ready for you guys next Friday!"

"We'll see about that, Bishop," they retorted! They all knew him.

One day Kari burst through the back door and exclaimed, "Guess who was working the TEC retreat? Bishop Dudley, and he is soooo great! He talks to each one of us as if we were the *only* one in the room! He's so full of energy and enthusiasm. I can't believe he's *retired!*"

The priesthood has taken quite a hit since it was revealed that a few sinful men used their positions to abuse youngsters in their charge. As a mother of thirteen, I can't imagine the devastation to the victims and families involved. We can only pray for healing and forgiveness.

Saint Thérèse of Lisieux (The Little Flower), the patron saint of missionaries, had a deep devotion and prayed daily for priests. And Archbishop Fulton J. Sheen often advised, "If we ever knew how busy the devil is trying to taunt and tempt priests, we would be on our knees praying for their spiritual protection."[1]

It is too soon to know if any vocations will come from this family. What I do know is that our children see priests and sisters as happy, healthy, vibrant witnesses who radiate their love of faith as they live out their vocational call.

So don't wait for your kids to be grown or your home to be perfect. Pick up the phone and invite a priest over for dinner! He'll love it, and so will you! 🌲

26

Christmas Memories

I thought it might be interesting to poll my kids about their memories of Christmases past. We parents have our own "vivid" recollections, but hearing a child's perspective is even better.

You can probably guess that, with our size family, there were no fond recollections of escapes to Disneyworld, Epcot or fun in the Florida sun! No. The trips our kids recall are those to the Christmas tree lot. Dad strategically planned these to occur just a few days before Christmas, when prices were slashed and the seller more sympathetic to a vanload of kids anxiously waiting to select the biggest evergreen they could find. Of course, Dad hesitated and haggled until the price was just right. That's John!

I will concede that there were occasions when our young would show twinges of envy over what "other kids got" to have or do at Christmas. I think it was Michael who came through the back door one year with a long face and announced, "Man, Ben's so lucky. He and his folks are spending Christmas at Disneyworld," or Florida, Cancun or some exotic place or another.

"The poor kid," I replied. "Don't you feel sorry for children who have no brothers and sisters to play with?

Their parents have to go *out of their way* to look for fun and adventure."

"Yeah, like I reeeeally feel sorry for Ben," Michael responded.

"Well, you kids don't need Disney. You have each other!"

"Don't remind me."

OK, so they weren't always thrilled about sharing their toys, trikes, bedrooms (at one time we had three sets of bunk beds) and lives with a houseful of siblings. Yet time and maturity have a wonderful way of mellowing a youthful perspective. When our daughter Angie served as maid of honor for her sister Mary Elizabeth, she raised her glass in a toast: "I just want to thank our parents, who had all of us kids so close together so we could grow up together and be such good friends."

Hmmmm. This was from the same girl who used to complain, "Mary doesn't even *ask* before she wears my clothes!"

Back to Christmas memories: Chrissy, our oldest, remembered the "stockings full of candy—except for Tony's, which always had a rotten potato."

Tony, on the other hand, only remembered the fun of getting up early on Christmas morning. "Waking Dad up and pulling him out of bed was always the challenge. We weren't allowed to go into the living room till he was up!"

In fact, *every* one of the kids recalled John's feigning sleepiness and pretending he needed to be dragged out of bed and helped down the stairs to a living room full of packages. "We even tried changing Dad's alarm clock to trick him into thinking it was later," Joseph said.

And there was always the empty milk glass and cookie plate with a note from Santa—with handwriting that looked more and more like Dad's as the kids grew older.

Caroling on Christmas Eve morning at Catholic Eldercare is one of Kari's favorite Christmas memories. "It is always so much fun to go there and see the people. You can tell by their faces how much they appreciate our coming."

For over twenty years the Kuharski family (now extended to our grown children and grandchildren) have teamed up with the Archambaults, our good friends and neighbors, to bring cookies and caroling to residents of local nursing homes. Mary Elizabeth remembers, "We kids worked for days and weeks getting ready for Christmas. We practiced our songs, rehearsed our routines (special skits for 'Rudolph the Red-Nosed Reindeer' and 'The Twelve Days of Christmas') and drew endless stacks of pictures to hand out with our homemade cookies to the nursing home residents. The anticipation was as much fun as doing it!"

The Christmas that stands out most for Chrissy is the year we returned home from midnight Mass and her boyfriend proposed to her. "Andy was so nervous all through Mass. Later I couldn't figure out why he wanted me to open his gift."

Then there were the handmade Christmas gifts for each other or pooling resources to get brothers and sisters "something they *really* wanted." Yet the most interesting thing about my little "family poll" is that none of our young mentioned a particular gift item or "something they'd always wanted" as a favorite Christmas memory. It was all about family and what *they* were giving and the fun and joy that permeated the atmosphere, crowded as it was!

And that's the point. No matter what the ad agencies try to sell us, the best Christmases we will ever have and those that will leave the fondest memories are the ones we give to others. It's not about money. It's more about time, about giving of ourselves with nothing expected in return.

Time spells LOVE. The simple things we do for others can have the most profound impact. Whether it's with the family or a loved one, a shut-in or someone who needs us, the gift of ourselves says to another, "I care about you."

As Christians we strive—not just at Christmastime but all year through—to see Christ in others and act accordingly. When we do that, they too will see him in us. 🌳

> "They shall name him Emmanuel," which means, "God is with us."
>
> —MATTHEW 1:23

27

Children: Blessings, Not Burdens!

I was recently asked to list "the blessings of having children" and, in particular, the "benefits of a large family." Hmmmm.

First I had to develop temporary amnesia. I didn't want to think about the one who was grounded at the time and telling us he "doesn't need parents anymore." Or about the time Mrs. Loomis from church told me two of my sons nominated me for president of the Mean Mothers Club!

Yes, there are challenges, but I was grateful for the opportunity to talk about one of the greatest gifts in my life: my children. Here are but a few of the blessings we have experienced:

Blessing 1: *A Reflection of God's Love*. The first thing that came to me as a first-time mother was an overwhelming sense of awe. I never *dreamed* something could touch me so profoundly. How could this little one, so fragile, so perfect, so intricately made, be created by anything or anyone other than a magnificent God? No grand "ooze" or split atom could produce such a masterpiece. And to think he was entrusting us with this precious little life!

Blessing 2: *A Reflection of My Spouse.* I see a glimpse of John in the features, traits and mannerisms of each of our "tummy" children. Sometimes it's laughable, other times downright maddening!

Even in our adopted young we see ourselves. They are *us* not by blood but by love and *osmosis!*

They too came to us as part of God's unique plan. It is no real surprise to occasionally hear one say, "Well, I'm like Dad in…." Or to hear my Vietnamese son Tony boast, "I'm like Grandpa Delmonico in that way." (Grandpa was full Italian.)

Most married couples see a similar reflection of their spouse in their young. These little "shadows" are gifts from a loving God—and the very result of their married love! "Your wife will be like a fruitful vine / within your house; / your children will be like olive shoots / around your table. / Thus shall the man be blessed / who fears the LORD" (Psalm 128:3–4).

Blessing 3: *A Sense of Wonder at Being "Cocreators" With God.* We are no longer just husband and wife, but through pregnancy we have been drawn up in a profound mystery. We are being permitted to *share* in the creative power of God! Miraculous when you think about it.

Blessing 4: *A Sense of Humor.* Who but a child can find laughter in even the smallest thing and can draw us out of our stuffy selves to appreciate the discovery? From the tiny infant who flashes a first frown at the taste of cooked carrots, to the toddler who insists on stepping in the puddle, to the teen who thinks *our* dress is laughable, there is humor in the everyday if we but only look!

Blessing 5: *A Sense of Humility (Ouch).* Whether it's a child's tantrum in the checkout lane at the grocery store, a visit from the neighbor who tells you your son picked all her green tomatoes or that dreaded phone call from the school principal, in one way or another children chip away at any semblance of pride we may cling to and help us embrace a sense of humility. This is a lesson I keep learning and relearning!

Blessing 6: *A Desire for Holiness*. Prayer and a need for God take on a whole new meaning once we become parents. We want *more* for our young than things. Something holy is going on here. We realize we want their happiness always, for all eternity. That's heaven. And once that becomes the focus and goal, we begin to *really* pray for the child and for ourselves. Children help us sort out and see the real priorities in life.

Blessing 7: *Love Multiplies!* Pity the young couples who intentionally remain childless or who limit themselves to one or two children, thinking they are unable to "divide their love" among many. I am not referring here to those who *can't* have children but those who *won't*, refusing to be open to God's gift.

This was one of the earliest lessons God taught ole skeptical me when we began to enlarge our family. When I was single and working as a legal secretary, I dreamed of saving my money to one day travel the globe. God did me one better. He gave me John, my Polish Prince, and brought the world to us. And with it came love with an international flavor that only God could have designed. He proved to me that love never divides; it only multiplies!

"What no eye has seen, nor ear heard, nor the human heart conceived, what God has prepared for those who love him" (1 Corinthians 2:9).

Blessing 8: *Someone to Share With*. Holidays, birthdays, vacations and fun times all seem better when shared with family. Friends and neighbors are wonderful, but it is our family we look to and lean on, especially during the biggest joys and the greatest trials. When things seem bleak, the love of a child can pull us up, keep us focused and head us back in the right direction.

Blessing 9: *Someone to Whom We Can Pass on Our Heritage.* If I had a sense of awe at the birth of my children, I had an overwhelming sense of gratitude when I set eyes on my first grandchild. She and the others to follow are living testimony of our married love, now passed to a new generation! No boat or trip, no wetland or rain forest can produce such a legacy.

Blessing 10: *Comfort and Companionship in Old Age.* One of my kids used to say, "You only have us so we can do all of the work" (someday he'll know!). But in a sense these children and grandchildren are the ones who will put smiles on our faces and brighten even our darkest days. When our hair has turned gray and we are sick or confined, it is they and their children who will bring us the greatest joy!

I am sure there are many more blessings one might list. These are just a few that come to mind. 🌿

> Our God is in the heavens;
>   he does whatever he pleases….
> The LORD has been mindful of us; he will bless us;…
> he will bless those who fear the LORD,
>   both small and great.
> May the LORD give you increase,
>   both you and your children.
> May you be blessed by the LORD,
>   who made heaven and earth.
>
> —PSALM 115:3, 12, 13–15

28

The Engagement Blessing

This is my commandment, that you love one another as I have loved you.

—John 15:12

Let me tell you about the year our daughter Angie became engaged to the "love of her life," Adam. How they met and the plans they made for their engagement and wedding were a great joy to watch for those of us on the "sidelines."

I'd like to tell you that I helped bring Angie and Adam together, but when I tell Angie that she just rolls her eyes and gives me one of those "Aren't you stretching it a bit?" looks. Well, you be the judge.

It all began when I learned of a wonderful opportunity for Angie (then eighteen) and her sister Kari (sixteen) to attend World Youth Day, which was being held in Paris, France. I got a less-than-enthusiastic response when I first told them about the pilgrimage to see the pope. I wasn't sure if their reluctance was based on the fact that they would have to pay for it out of their own savings, earned from part-time jobs. Or if, as they later confessed, they feared the ten-day trip would be nothing more than a nonstop tour of Paris churches and endless rosaries along the way!

Luckily, an anonymous donor sweetened the prospect by offering to pay a large portion of each girl's expenses. And so Angie and Kari were off to Paris with twenty-five other teens from the Minneapolis–St. Paul area.

When the girls returned from the pilgrimage, they bubbled with excitement about all that they had seen and done. There were tours through some of the great palaces and churches of Paris, an outdoor Mass near the Eiffel Tower, one night sleeping under the stars and the "awesome" (as the kids would say) opportunity to be in the presence of Pope John Paul II.

In addition to coming home with backpacks full of photos and souvenirs, they had forged friendships with many of their young travel companions—and guess who was one of them? A tall, good-looking, eighteen-year-old blond named Adam.

Now, don't I deserve some credit on this one?

Initially Angie and Adam saw each other only in "follow-up" get-togethers, but when Adam finally called our house and asked for Angie, she lit up brighter than John's front yard Christmas light display. Soon they were attending each other's school dances and sharing special occasions with family and friends.

The first year of college they attended different schools, but Angie was so homesick (I was dumb enough at first to think she missed us!), she switched schools to be close to home and you-know-who. The challenges of holding down part-time jobs and keeping focused on their education brought them a sense of maturity and sureness. Finally graduation came and their entrance into the work force—with both of them resolved to pay off remaining college loans. They were in love but determined to do things in the right order.

Angie was maid of honor for her sister Mary Elizabeth that year, and this only heightened the anticipation for her and Adam. Siblings and friends chided, "You guys are next, aren't you?" But they were prudent, waiting until marriage seemed affordable.

One fall day, as I worked frantically in a misty cold rain to bed down my roses for the winter and put away the remaining flowerpots, there stood a beaming Adam under the clothes pole. When he saw John saunter up the back walk from the garage, he quickly blurted out (before he lost his courage, he later said), "Well, now that I have you two together, there is something I want to ask you. I would like your permission to ask your daughter to marry me."

His hand reached inside his pocket, pulling out a small box. He popped open the top with his shaking fingers to show off the beautiful diamond ring he planned to present to Angie.

Of course we said yes. The match seemed as perfect as the diamond he had chosen. Here's a guy who fits like a glove in our family. What a blessing!

That evening Adam and Angie attended a special Emmy Awards event. A video profile that Angie had done for a college communication course had been nominated for an award. She didn't win the Emmy, but the real prize came soon after.

Adam knelt down in the lobby of the busy ballroom to propose marriage. It's quite a feat to catch Angie, the "queen of right planning and coordinating," by surprise, but that he did! When she returned home that night, she floated through the front door holding her left hand out for all to see.

"I knew it would happen someday, but when it did, it was more exciting and wonderful than I ever thought possible. Even after we've dated for so long and known each other so well, I feel like our engagement is something special," Angie confided later.

Before Angie and Adam were swept up in the busyness of wedding plans, they called Father Tollefson, the associate priest at St. Charles's, and arranged to have their engagement blessed. I hadn't seen this done since John and I had our own engagement blessed many years ago. How wonderful to witness it anew in the life of one of our children!

Thus, on a beautiful Sunday morning in November, Angie and Adam, surrounded by parents, brothers, sisters, nieces and nephews, stood before Father at the steps of the altar to receive his blessing: "Let us pray, then, for God's blessing to come upon this couple, our brother and sister: that as they await the day of their wedding, they will grow in mutual respect and in their love for one another; that through their companionship and prayer together they will prepare themselves rightly and chastely for marriage."

After two short Scripture readings and intercessory prayers, Father concluded with: "Lord God, the source of all love, the wise plan of your providence has brought these young people together. As they prepare themselves for the sacrament of marriage and pray for your grace, grant that, strengthened by your blessing, they may grow in their respect for one another and cherish each other with a sincere love."

The Catholic church urges a profound reverence for the sacrament of marriage. The Order for the Blessing of an Engaged Couple states, "The betrothal of a young Christian couple therefore is a special occasion for their families, who should celebrate it together with prayer and a special rite. In this way they ask God's blessing that the happiness promised by the children's engagement will be brought to fulfillment."

And celebrate we did! What a great occasion for both families to come together in loving support of our children!

Hopefully more young couples will seek this blessing. It is not only a wonderful way to begin an engagement but a visible reminder to one and all of God's presence in the covenant to come.

> And now faith, hope, and love abide, these three; and the greatest of these is love.
>
> —1 CORINTHIANS 13:13

29

"Thanks, Mr. President!"

Many impressions and memories have surfaced in the wake of the death of President Ronald Reagan, who is now said to be one of the most popular American presidents in modern time.

I have no lofty insight as to his leadership or political skills. While he faced formidable foes and the stalemate of a Cold War, we had our hands full with the simple daily routine of diapers, dishes and assorted dispositions of a growing household of children.

It was comforting then to know that President Reagan was handling the threat of a missile crisis and charming Mikhail Gorbachev into putting an end to the decades-old Cold War, while I had all I could do haggling with my HMO over a kid's recurring bout with malaria—yes, I said "malaria"—and another's need for personalized care that didn't quite fit the mold of their wellness coverage. The only brush I had with foreign countries was the struggle to pass the necessary medical and visa requirements for our adopted children. Two came from orphanages in Vietnam, one from the Philippines and another from India. That was enough "red tape" and intrigue for us!

But my rule for measuring the greatness of an individual is not firmness or finesse in preventing war or negotiating peace. Others have done as well. Even an uncanny ability to connect and communicate with a diverse people is not the mark of true greatness. Rather, I believe, the sign of greatness is when a leader shows true compassion and concern for the "little guy"—the one who may never vote for him, root for him or be able to return the favor. A small act of kindness may make no headline or tip the popularity polls, but it truly shows the greatness of an individual.

Ronald Reagan was pro-life as president, when he could have sidestepped the issue or taken the more comfortable "personally opposed but" position. His outspoken opposition to legal abortion made good sense to this household, half of whom some would consider to be unplanned, imperfect or unwanted.

But the real proof of his concern for the "little guy" came home clearly the year we discovered that one of our sons needed hearing aids in both ears. Already struggling with cerebral palsy, speech difficulties from a cleft palate, emotional adjustments to his new family in America and the sudden hormonal changes of adolescence, Vincent was refusing to wear his hearing aids. Then I saw a story in the *Minneapolis Star* about President Reagan's use of a hearing aid. I encouraged Vincent to write him. I slipped in a note describing Vincent's embarrassment by the cumbersome aids. He was miffed that the President's aids were smaller and less visible than those he was required to wear.

The response we received was far better than I could have imagined. One letter was to my husband and me:

November 28, 1983

Dear Mr. and Mrs. Kuharski,

Thank you very much for your letter, your kind words and prayers. More than that, thank you for what you are doing with your lives and for so many others. I've had some contact with other families like yours and know the love that fills your home and surrounds you.

I'm enclosing a note to Vincent. My ear problem is the result of a shooting accident. No wound—the gun just went off right by my ear. Over the years the nerves in the inner ear deteriorated with the result— a loss of much of the hearing in that ear. I wanted you to know because it is my understanding that various types of hearing aids are designed for different types of deafness. Vincent would probably have to be examined to see if this inside-the-ear amplifier would solve his problem.

My note to him is aimed at encouraging him to accept his problem. I hope it will help. In the meantime, the name of the company which makes mine is _____. Again, thanks and God bless you.

Sincerely,
Ronald Reagan

The president's letter to Vincent was handwritten:

Dear Vincent,

I've sent the name and address of the hearing aid company to your parents. Those of us who have hearing problems sometimes have to have different types of aids depending on what causes our problem.

I know how you feel about the aids you wear behind your ears, but if that's the kind you need, wear them and be happy they help you hear.

When I was your age I learned I couldn't see as well as other people and had to have glasses. They weren't quite as common then as they've become in recent years. I was very self-conscious and embarrassed about wearing glasses, but believe me, I outgrew that and learned to be happy because with them I could see all the beauty I'd been missing. Now it's glasses and a hearing aid, and I think I'm pretty lucky.

Best wishes to you, and God bless you.
Ronald Reagan

Thanks, Mr. President. Our prayers go with you. 🌲

30

God's Children
by Adoption

> See what love the Father has given us, that we should
> be called children of God; and that is what we are.
> The reason the world does not know us is that it did
> not know him. Beloved, we are God's children now;
> what we will be has not yet been revealed. What we
> do know is this: when he is revealed, we will be like
> him, for we will see him as he is. And all who have
> this hope in him purify themselves, just as he is pure.
> —1 JOHN 3:1–3

One of our family's favorite hymns is "Sing Praise to
our Creator." It's not the melody but the words that mean
so much. In truth it's the phrase "God's children by adoption" that comes "alive" in this household, with seven out
of fifteen of us adopted.

"God has *his* ways of bringing children and parents
together," I've often told our young. One way is Plan A or
"tummy" (as the kids would say). The other is Plan B or
adoption. We've been blessed to experience both plans.

"All who are led by the Spirit of God are children of
God. For you did not receive a spirit of slavery to fall back
into fear, but you have received a spirit of adoption. When
we cry, 'Abba! Father!' it is that very Spirit bearing witness
with our spirit that we are children of God" (Romans 8:14).

I feel sorry for couples who would eagerly adopt but
are prevented because of the astronomical costs and the

scarcity of babies. An anti-adoption mindset convinces millions of unwed mothers each year to abort or keep their
babies rather than consider the goodness of adoption.

Certainly adoption isn't for everyone, but we felt led
by *Someone* greater than we! It became our vocational call,
and we can't imagine what our marriage and lives would
have been like had we said no to that call.

"The desire to adopt is like a burning coal in my
heart," I would tell my occasionally hesitant husband. The
only "burning" he was feeling was in his wallet! Prayer,
patience and *persistence* always seemed to bring balance
when our family planning visions were not in unison.

Granted, that sense of *vocation* may have escaped us
when we were rocking little ones to sleep after nightmares,
disciplining erratic behavior—temper tantrums, spitting,
biting and throwing food, to name but a few—or stretching
a bulging budget to accommodate Catholic school tuition,
hearing aids, medical needs, one more set of braces or
glasses. But we were hooked.

Our adopted children enriched our lives in many
ways. They brought us to our knees and helped us stay
God-centered. We learned to lean on him for grace and all
our needs. Their mere presence reminded us daily of the
real meaning and purpose of life!

My husband is full Polish, and I come from an Italian
background. Our children came from far and near. "It's a
mini-United Nations!" our mailman used to say, as we
began to blend a variety of colors and cultures, creating
our own personal "melting pot." We learned to adjust,
adapt and accept each others' backgrounds and biases,
not to mention the biggest bugaboo of all: behaviors and
temperaments! Our family came to experience with
poignancy Saint Paul's words, "There is no longer Jew or

Greek, there is no longer slave or free, there is no longer male and female; for all of you are one in Christ Jesus" (Galatians 3:28).

We also encountered prejudice. Etched forever in our minds is the day that our black-skinned son Charlie, then twelve, was beaten up by a gang of white teens while on his daily paper route. After the police left and we gathered in prayer at the dinner table, trying to create an atmosphere of calm, it was Charlie who taught us a lesson in forgiveness. He prayed, "Dear Jesus, please forgive those boys. I know they just don't know any better."

Most of our adopted children were beyond infancy when they came to our home, and most arrived with physical, mental or emotional challenges. In the severe and in the small we saw that we could do little. One child's history of abandonment and abuse prevented him from ever accepting family life and love, no matter how hard we tried. He still reminds us of our human frailty and of the need to continue to rely on God's mercy.

Yes, we had our share of testing and trials—perhaps more than other families simply because of our numbers. Through it all we sensed that God had his eye on our "sparrows." "Even the sparrow finds a home, / and the swallow a nest for herself, / where she may lay her young" (Psalm 84:3).

Psalm 139 reminds us, "It was you who formed my inward parts; / you knit me together in my mother's womb. / I praise you, for I am fearfully and wonderfully made. / Wonderful are your works; / that I know very well."

In other words, we know that *God makes no mistakes!* There is no such thing as an "unwanted child." God has a purpose and a plan for each of us. We are *all*, as the song says, "God's children by adoption."

What's it like at our house now, with most of the children grown and on their own? Five are married, and we have twelve grandchildren. The graduations, holidays, weddings, special events and Sunday dinners are what gather us together and keep us up-to-date and "united."

Did color, culture or adoption prevent closeness? To the contrary and in spite of the obvious distinctions to outsiders, we *live* and *love* as one family. As one of our little ones once asked, "Which of us are adopted? I forget!"

> Blessed be the God and Father of our Lord Jesus Christ, who has blessed us in Christ with every spiritual blessing in the heavenly places, just as he chose us in Christ before the foundation of the world to be holy and blameless before him in love. He destined us for adoption as his children through Jesus Christ.
> —EPHESIANS 1:3–5

31

A Father's View

I will be your father, and you shall be my sons and daughters, says the Lord Almighty.

—2 CORINTHIANS 6:18

What are a father's feelings and fears regarding the adoption process? The following is an interview with John Kuharski, father of thirteen children, six of whom are adopted:

When you first adopted, you already had two children born to you. Why did you decide to add to your family through adoption?

My first thought at the time was, because there were kids in this world without parents and a home, brothers and sisters. I felt we had the ability to provide for more children, not just financially but also with love and a good moral foundation.

I found out later that this "savior" mentality was only half correct. We weren't just doing something for these kids. *They* were doing something for us!

Through the adoption process my wife and I discovered more about each other. We were able to share the anticipation and excitement, the unknown, the thoughts and feelings of who we are and just why we are doing what we're doing. It was something we were doing together, in total agreement. The adopted kids provided us an opportunity to look at our own goals and path to the future.

As spouses in our culture were walking out on each other and talking about "me," we were planning in terms of "US." There was a wonderful sense of purpose, direction and unity.

What made you feel comfortable with the thought of adopting?

My wife was adopted, and my older sister had an adopted child. But more than that, I believe that all children come from God. Though I didn't plant the seed and my wife didn't conceive and nurture it, we knew God put our adopted children on this earth to be loved and cared for. Both Mary Ann and I felt sure that we could offer that love and care to an adopted child.

Did you have any reservations or second thoughts?

One reservation was financial. Could I provide for a large family adequately, not only when they were young but all the way through to college?

Also, would I be able to spend the amount of time with each of them that a father should? Would I be a good example to them—morally, emotionally and personally— so that they would grow up to become good Catholic men and women?

I wondered if I would love and care for the adopted kids in the same manner as the children who were born from our union. Would I treat any of them differently because they didn't look like me? Would I be as proud to have them in my family?

I remember thinking about our adopted kids' teenage years and wondering, "Will they be comfortable with kids of the opposite sex and of a different culture when they begin dating and socializing? Will they have the opportunity to marry and have their own families? Will our adoption of them help or hurt?"

What we discovered was just how secure these children are. Our adopted children's dating and social opportunities were just as numerous and "normal" as the other kids'. They chose their friends and dates not by the color of their skin (many had dates with blacks and Asians, as well as whites) but by their code of conduct. Isn't that what every parent wants their children to be able to do?

What was it like to go through the adoption process?

The adoption process is NOT easy; in fact, it is very difficult. There seemed to be endless forms to complete, meetings to attend, waiting and then more waiting. And there were many disappointments along the way, such as when the process was delayed.

The waiting made me think of the child out there who was already born, perhaps living in an orphanage, who should be with a loving family but instead was *waiting* just as we were. The child may have been suffering, lonely, lying for hours in a crib without proper care or loving attention. It made me more determined.

With adoption I felt like a real participant in the whole process. With Mary Ann's pregnancies—as wonderful as they were—I could not experience the feeling of new life inside. I was only an observer during labor and delivery. And I couldn't nurse the baby after the birth! But with our adopted children we went through the "labor and delivery" together. There were the paperwork, the meetings, the waiting, the anticipation, the eagerness and finally the excitement that the child was finally becoming ours! It was a growing and very moving experience.

Tell us more about the effect adoption had on your relationship with your wife.

I think adopting had a very positive effect on our marriage relationship. In the beginning stages the process involved a lot of discussion: "Should we, or shouldn't we?" "Can we care for and love someone else's child as well as we do our own?" "Can we financially support a larger family?" We shared our innermost feelings and even our fears and frustrations about children and about our goals and plans for the future. These discussions brought us closer together.

As the waiting and delays occurred, there seemed to be an even more determined "unity of spirit" in what we were doing. It was something *WE* were resolved to do, and it would be beneficial to *ALL* of us.

And then, when the child finally came, there was the shared excitement and joy over this precious new member of our family. We shared everything from tears to jokes as we grew to love children who looked unlike those born to us. It was a wonderful and really unexplainable experience.

Did you think about how adoption would affect your other children?

My hope was that our other kids would see the adopted children as their brothers and sisters and not just as people staying at our house for a period of time, such as in foster care. I was always *amazed* at how well they received the adopted child, treating him or her as part of the family and sharing toys and belongings. In some respects I think our kids adapted more quickly than we did. We were too concerned with how all of it was going to fit together.

I believe the children's adjustment happened so naturally because Mary Ann and I shared the adoption process and procedure with them, so they were involved from the beginning.

Was there a concern about how your adopting would affect the extended family?

There was some concern, especially on my wife's side of the family. Her parents felt that because we had our *own* children, why adopt—especially children from other parts of the world. They accepted our first two adoptions but had problems with our third because of the darkness of his skin. We didn't tell them about the last three adoptions until the child came. It was easier on us that way. We thought it would be difficult for them to reject a cute little face, which it was!

One family member told her children that our adopted kids were *not* their cousins. She didn't want her kids to become friends with our adopted ones. She got her wish, but she and her family were the losers, not us. Racism does exist and we had a taste of it—from the inside and out!

My mother would always say, "You guys are crazy!" when we told her about our plans to adopt another. Of course, she also thought we were "crazy" when we told her we were going to have another biological child. In either case she *always* was there for us and accepted each the minute he or she arrived.

There was some concern on my part about how our neighbors would accept our adopting children of a minority race and whether they would allow their children to socialize with ours.

And would our children's classmates accept them? As it worked out, our adopted children had as many friends and opportunities as the others. Some even had more just because of their outgoing natures and involvements.

What was it like when your adopted child arrived? What were your feelings?

With Tina, our first adopted child, the first feeling was "Is she *really* coming?" We had waited so long, and there were so many delays.

There was a sense of mystery. What would she look like? What would she bring to our lives?

There were feelings of excitement. Many of our friends and family members were there when Tina arrived. There was such joy at welcoming home this little one, truly God's child.

Then there was a sense of accomplishment. We really did what we said we were going to do! She was now *ours* for the rest of our lives! Wow! Now the next step was to carry this out successfully!

And there were also the fears: "What did we do?" "Did we do the right thing?" "Can we be good parents to this little one?"

Interestingly, even after we became "experienced" as adoptive parents, those same feelings occurred all over again with each child. Each child brought indescribable mystery, excitement and, yes, fear!

Was the adjustment to a new child easier or more difficult than you expected?

The adjustment was definitely easier than expected. Yes, there were trying days with doctor visits, food adjustments and emotional outbursts, but nothing was intolerable or permanent. Our adopted children seemed to bond quickly, first to the other children and then to us. Probably it took longer for them to bond with my wife and me because they had been taken care of by various adults who were then taken out of their lives, which weakened their ability to attach and trust.

Our son Charlie was five and a half years old when he arrived. He was very dark-skinned, as compared with our white and Asian kids. I'll never forget the first bath I gave him. He really looked dark in that white tub! It seemed at first strange and then so fleeting, as it was only a matter of days before we were absolutely in love with him.

I remember Charlie's first Christmas pageant at St. Charles School. He was an angel, and Mary Ann dressed him in an old white sheet tied at the waist. She made white wings with gold around the edges and a halo for his head. His last words to us before he went on stage with his class were "Now, look for me in the back row. I'll be the angel on the left side of the room."

How could we miss him? He was the *only* black child in the pageant that year. He didn't get it, but Mary Ann and I loved it!

What about the risk in adopting those with "special needs"? Were their problems less or more serious than expected, and how did you handle them?

"Special needs" can be broken into three areas: physical, mental and emotional. Many of the physical conditions were easily rectified because of the medical and educational resources available to us. Some of the children needed extensive dental care; others, hearing aids.

The mental needs were also a concern. We had access to special education resources and tutors to assist with learning disabilities and motor coordination.

The emotional needs were sometimes more serious and difficult, because you can't get into children's heads and understand or *fix* what they are thinking. Therapy can be long and involved, and we learned that it doesn't always help.

There is a sense of "mission" and accomplishment that comes with adopting a child with "special needs" and helping remove some of the hurdles in his or her life. Even though this involved doctors and money with varying results, we felt that it was a unique privilege.

What about disappointments? One of your adopted children, after a five-year struggle on your part, failed to bond with the family. Was there a lesson there?

Before this adoption we naïvely believed that all it takes is love and faith for *any adoption* to be successful. Love will *always* cure and heal hurts, we thought. We were wrong.

It seemed that the more we showed our love and support to one of our children, the more he would lash out, getting into deeper trouble at home, at school and in the neighborhood. He was fighting and stealing. We couldn't trust him to behave properly around our other children— or *any* small children. We were heartsick.

We sought psychiatric care for him and counseling for us, in an attempt to heal the wounds his acting up had caused. He was hospitalized for mental health problems twice, for months at a time, and eventually was court-ordered to a shelter for young boys. We stuck with him, hoping that he would finally believe, "I am loved. They are sticking with me and believe I can change and be good."

Yet his threats to the children and even to Mary Ann only increased. This child seemed to literally recoil at the prospect of having an emotional bond with others.

We now know that not *all* children are adoptable by families. Some have been too wounded and scarred to adapt to family life. Others, if they are older and have abuse in their history, should *never* be placed with a family of younger children who could become victims.

After five *long years* and his repeated threats, we finally relented to this boy's request and relinquished adoption. He was placed in a group foster home, and he remained there for approximately three years before he was legally on his own.

The lessons here are obvious:

- Always deal with a reputable orphanage and agency. Obviously the one in his homeland was not.

- Always get as complete a history as possible with regard to an older child.

- Every day is important in a child's life. The older the child, the less opportunity adopting parents have to share, shape and love. The younger the child, the greater the opportunity to bond and belong to one another.

There were other disappointments and hurdles we could not overcome. Still, we knew we were doing what God had called us to do. We planted the seeds of faith and love in each one. The rest is in God's hands.

Did you see a spiritual side to your adoptions?

Yes. The spiritual side was being able to put our trust and faith in God and believe that this was the right thing to do. We had to believe we would be successful because it was part of God's plan for us and these children. After all, we were now responsible, both physically and morally, for other individuals.

Adoption also made us realize that we could not accomplish the task of being good parents without God's help. This brought us closer to God in prayer and in our need to stay close to his sacraments.

What advice would you give to other fathers contemplating adoption?

Prayer is first and foremost. That will build your faith and trust in God. You need his grace to be a good father and provide personally, financially and morally for your family.

Next is agreement between both husband and wife. You both must believe this is right for YOU! There is an issue of timing here. Sometimes one is ready but the other is not. This doesn't necessarily mean "No" but maybe "Later," when both husband and wife are prepared and comfortable with the decision. You don't move ahead until BOTH are ready. My wife says this agreement comes with prayer and patience!

Third, I would suggest you take a step back, look at your family and try to picture your future. If you can say an unhesitating "Yes" to a question such as, "Will our holidays, our home and so on be better with the adoption of a child?" then you are ready to adopt, because you already believe it will enhance your lives for the better.

Fourth, if you have older children, it is good to involve them in the discussion and perhaps the decision, never giving them "veto" power but allowing them to give input. We found that, in one particular incident, God spoke quite clearly to us through one of our older children about whether or not we should move ahead with an adoption.

Once we made the decision to adopt, then came the waiting. This turned to anticipation and eagerness. Finally came the excitement and joy! In the end we would discover that WE NEEDED this child.

Finally, don't worry about the short-term events. It's funny how hindsight shows us that we spend far too much time and energy worrying about things—most of which *never* happen or are far less serious than we thought they would be. With prayer and the Lord behind you, everything will work out in the long run! 🌲

> We know that God makes all things work together
> for the good of those who love him.
>
> —ROMANS 8:28

32

The Adventure Begins

Our parenting began with Christine Ann. John seemed a *natural* at being a father. He would bound through the door each evening, pecking me on the cheek as he rushed by and headed straight for the bassinet and his seven-pound princess. He was smitten in his new role as father.

I readily dropped my career as a legal secretary to assume the vocation of at-home mom and all that it entailed. After all, there was an added purpose to our union. But I was a nervous wreck! How was I to take on this vital new role and do it successfully?

The worst advice seemed to come from the trendy books on parenting I picked up, most of which were written by "experts" with no kids. The best came with *time* and the wise support of my saintly pediatrician, a grandfatherly figure who lovingly guided me through the infancy of our first two children before his retirement.

"Prayer and common sense are your greatest helpmates," Dr. Lawrence Richdorf counseled. And he was right. His is the best advice I can offer any new parent today, adopting or otherwise!

Chrissy seemed to draw us even closer in some mysterious way, as we shared her discoveries and firsts. Never mind the cloth diapers, colicky disposition and pinched budget. She was pure gift!

Our irresistible first made us yearn for another. She coaxed us on in the exciting, enthralling, energy-sapping adventure known as *parenting.* In the next few chapters is a capsule view of that adventure. I want to tell you who the Kuharski kids are and where they are today.

Chrissy, the Big Sister

Our first child eagerly embraced her role of big sister, teacher and "leader of the pack." Her most endearing quality was the love and affection she so freely gave to her younger brothers and sisters. So thrilled was she when we adopted Tina and Tony, she wanted to show them off to *everyone.* One day she burst out the door of her kindergarten class, asking, "Since Melissa brought her cat for Show and Tell, why can't I bring my new baby brother and sister so everyone can see what we got at our house?"

From the beginning the words *caring* and *sharing* were written all over Chrissy. In first grade the children were each given a giant-sized cookie with M & M candies sprinkled over the top. Instead of eating hers, she brought it home to share with her little sister and brothers, all of whom gobbled their morsels whole with nary a glance of gratitude in return. Chrissy didn't care. She was pleased they had a taste.

Chrissy had more responsibility, more chores, more limitations and less freedom, by the sheer fact that I needed her help more than the others'. Yet she never resented the challenges. Rather, she said, "I thought it was great!"

When she was only seven, we learned of a little eight-year-old girl from Vietnam who was in need of an adoptive family. As we knelt to pray about God's direction, I could see Chrissy visibly choking back tears. Finally she blurted out, "It's not that I don't want to have her come into our family; it's just that then I won't be the *oldest*, and I like being the oldest." We never pursued that adoption, sensing that her burst of tears was God's answer.

After graduating from college, Chrissy fulfilled her childhood dream and became a third-grade teacher. She is now married to Andy, who blends in with our crew as if he'd always belonged. Chrissy is an active at-home mother of six children: Lizzie, eleven; Anne Marie, nine; Carolyn, six; James, five; John Paul, three; and baby Thomas. An expert seamstress (in her spare time), she even made the bridesmaid and flower girl dresses for her sister Mary's wedding. In addition, Chrissy is active with church and the pro-life effort.

> Train children in the right way,
>   and when old, they will not stray.
>
> —PROVERBS 22:6

Then Came Tim

Tim arrived two years after Chrissy, and my first fear was that "I'll never be able to love this child the way I loved the first." (I discovered years later that such a fear haunts many a mother before the arrival of a new child.) From the moment the little bundle bursting with activity was placed on my tummy, I was hooked.

The opposite of Chrissy with her programmed and perfect ways, Timmy was Mr. Mischief-in-the-Making. He managed to bust more knickknacks and collectibles than any other child and scare us silly by wandering off and getting lost. Yet I was in LOVE with the most charming, precocious child I'd ever laid eyes on!

Until Tim came on the scene, my home and my schedule ran like clockwork. I was nearing perfection, or so I thought, but God took care of that bad habit with the gift of one energetic kid. One year he pulled our Christmas tree over THREE times in a week. Yes, Tim was into EVERY-THING and had a sweet tooth, bar none! It was this child who taught me how to relax and rethink my priorities about handprints on tables.

In his teen years Tim began to challenge some of our rules. He worked hard nights and weekends at a local gas station to help pay for Catholic high school and college. Thus he was sure he was "old enough to set my own hours." Not in this house.

Always obedient and respectful, our stand-offs were memorable but few. One night he came in past curfew and there I stood. I promptly confiscated his car keys (he owned the car and paid his own insurance). This twenty year old would be walking or taking the bus for a few weeks.

My most cherished memory of Tim is of his loving and open response at age five to our adoption of Charlie, who was only six months older than Tim and didn't speak a word of English. Tim offered his love and friendship to this new brother, sharing his room, his toys and even his friends. He was a wonderful brother and role model to Charlie and the others who followed.

After college Tim, like his father, went into account-ing. He is now married to Tina, a beautiful young woman with a warm and loving personality, and they have three beautiful children, Nick (five), Lauren (two) and Justin (2 months).

One of the greatest thrills I received as a grandmother was the night Tim called to tell me of Nicholas's birth. His voice cracked with emotion as he tried to announce the good news. "Mom, we have a baby," he said in a barely audible voice. "It's so unbelievable!"

And now he knows: There is no greater blessing than the gift of a child! 🌲

33

Tina and Tony Fly In

Very truly, I tell you, if you ask anything of the Father
in my name, he will give it to you.

—JOHN 16:23

Deciding to adopt brought a mixture of emotion. While I freely admit it was my idea, when it came to the months of waiting it was John who seemed more steady, with few doubts and little anxiety. I was haunted by the concern, "Will I be able to love this child as I do the others?" Lucky for me, John was "full speed ahead."

And ironically it was John's folks, with their scant experience with adoption, who were most supportive of our desire to adopt a "hard-to-place" child. My folks, on the other hand, thought we'd lost our minds! Here they were, successful parents of three adopted children, but because the child was coming from foreign shores with a questionable medical history, they were *not* excited.

Later we suffered a painful break with my parents when we adopted a black child. It took months on my mother's part and years for my dad to accept what we had done. My father grew up in a poor Italian neighborhood where racial prejudice was the norm. "The lighter the Italian, the easier you're accepted," he would confide.

The turning point came when Dad called one day needing help at his hobby farm. He sheepishly asked, "I hear your boys are getting big. Are they old enough to bale some hay and clean out a barn?"

"They sure are, Dad," I responded. It was an ice-breaker and a beginning. By the end of that summer the boys were making weekly trips to Grandpa's farm, creating fond memories that remain with them to this day.

I reveal this not to detract from the good parents I had but merely to acknowledge that sometimes there is opposition in a family. It is healthy for the couple to be aware of this, talk about it and then decide with prayer what is right *for them.* Had we listened to the advice of my parents or some outsiders, we never would have adopted even one child, and I can't bear to think what our lives would have been like without them!

Nurse Tina

We applied for adoption when Chrissy was three and Tim, one. We thought the paperwork and wait would never end. Our application was delayed by martial law in the Philippines, and our home study was lost twice, once in a flood. At that point our caseworker suggested we "give up the idea of the Philippine adoption and apply for a Korean."

But by then we had a tiny photo of Tina on our bedroom nightstand. She lay on a small blanket atop a tile floor in the Manila orphanage. Not much for hair, she displayed a definite "lump" on the back of her head, sign of a possible cephal hematoma, which the orphanage had mentioned in her "bio sketch." We found her adorable, and we would wait through *ten* floods and *ten* more home studies if we had to!

Finally, after waiting over a year, Tina Marie, at eighteen months, received a visa to come to America. Her flight arrived at 6:20 A.M., and I don't think I slept a wink the last few days before her arrival. She came dressed in a summer frock and a stocking cap. She was gorgeous! I cried with joy all the way home.

John could hardly take his eyes off of her. He grasped the steering wheel with one hand and patted her reassuringly with the other. "Boy, I can't believe we're so lucky," he kept saying as we drove across town toward home. "I thought *we* were supposed to be doing something for *her*, but I think *she* is the one who is doing something for us."

Reality set in within the next twenty-four hours, as we discovered that her nights were our days. She was alert through the night, wanting to eat, while during the day a Mack truck driving through her bedroom would not have disturbed her! Topping that, she resented her new home and family. She spit, bit the other children, threw food and spun tantrums like no one else could.

In spite of the shaky start, we learned through Tina how easy it was to open our hearts to a child who was not "flesh of our flesh" or "bone of our bone." I called her my "Rosebud" because initially she was so closed to our affection, but when she began to "unfold," her beauty and warmth could radiate throughout a room.

Tina was our daredevil—the first to surfboard and water-ski—and an overachiever. She pushed herself to be the best at whatever she chose to do, whether it was playing the piano or shooting a basketball. The kids called her "The Nurse" because, while the others feigned sick stomachs at the mere thought of bruises and blood, Tina could have someone washed, wrapped and walking before the tears were dry!

In her growing-up years Tina was my "kitchen aide." She loved to cook alongside Mom, and cooking is still one of her favorite pastimes.

Tina is now married to Steve and is living her childhood

dream, working as a registered nurse in Minneapolis. And to think we would have missed this little "Rosebud" if we'd let the frustration of floods and lost home studies change our minds!

Tony, the Miracle

Chalk this one up to my impatience and John's naïveté. "As long as things are taking so long with Tina's adoption," I reasoned to John, "and it's been well over a year already, why not get the paperwork rolling to adopt from Vietnam?"

"Yep, we might as well start now," he agreed. "Everything seems to take *years*."

Surprise, surprise! We had a picture referral just four weeks after our home study was flown over, and Baby Tony would be in our home three weeks after that!

We believe to this day that it was God's providence that saved our baby's life. The prospect for Vietnamese orphans during those war years was not good: 80 percent of the infants died within their first year. There was no one to cuddle, hold and love these babies. When there is no one who cares, a baby's *will* to live withers and dies.

It was two days after Tina's homecoming, and we had just arrived home from taking her to the doctor for a thorough exam. *All* of us were showing signs of exhaustion with our new "midnight screamer." The phone rang, and an accented voice on the other end identified herself as calling from Air France. She insisted that "your son is boarding his flight and will be arriving in New York City in two days." We thought it was a joke, but the joke was on us!

Tony, whom we instantly tagged our "miracle baby," came thanks to a government-issued emergency medical visa. Only twenty babies from Vietnam received such status that Christmas week. This probably saved Tony's frail young life.

His needs were urgent. He was two months old and weighed a scant five pounds, suffering, as the medical report stated, from "malnutrition, starvation, diarrhea and severe dehydration." The report concluded, "Child will not survive orphanage life." We were warned of the possibility of other "undiagnosed medical risks," such as hearing loss and mental retardation.

Tony was the baby who never cried. He had learned in his young life that crying brought no response. It was a scary thing to have a little one so frail and fragile and only to be able to *guess* at his needs because he never let out a whimper. Having lived through two colicky infants and now adjusting to "Tantrum Tina," I never thought I'd wish to hear a baby cry, but that is exactly what I wished for Tony.

Those first months I strapped Tony to me, carrying him in front-pack fashion almost everywhere. It was easier to keep an eye on him than to worry that he might stop breathing. At night we placed him next to my bed in the top of a baby buggy, where I could reach over and put my hand on him throughout the night to make sure of his feeble yet rhythmic breathing.

Tony's progress was truly miraculous. By the time he was three and a half, he was walking, running, climbing and curious like every other child his age. Our only concern was his lack of language. Not a word came from his mouth. Rather, he pointed toward whatever he was after, emitting a grunt or a groan until he got our attention. As he hedged toward four, I was sure there was a serious disability.

"Let's not jump to conclusions," John would say reassuringly. "Let's take him to the doctor and see what the problem is."

That we did. But first I prayed that God would give me vision for this child and help me accept any disabilities he might have. More importantly, I prayed that God would help *me* learn how to *help him*. And I prayed that if it was God's will that Tony speak, he would show me a sign. "Just let him say *ONE WORD,* Lord, so I know there is a chance for progress."

Our pediatrician recommended a specialist. After extensive tests the psychologist, a kindly older woman, advised, "Your little boy appears normal in every way. There seems to be no reason for his inability to talk. Just maybe as the fourth child in the family, he's never felt the *need* to talk. He's been able to get everything he wants with a simple grunt or groan."

Hmmmm.

Within a week after my prayer and our doctor visits, Tony uttered his first word, "cookie," as he pointed to our windowed oven, anxiously waiting for the freshly baked batch. When I heard the word, the tears ran uncontrollably down my cheeks. God is so good!

Once Tony began talking, he never quit. The kids used to call him "Motormouth."

From toddler to teen, Tony was into *everything*— except schoolwork, household chores and responsibility. Tony will be the first to say he "holds the record" when it comes to losing privileges for stinky behavior. "I remember all the times the teacher would call from school," he laughingly recalls. "When I'd walk in the back door, Mom would have a list of chores a *mile long* waiting for me. I should have known I wasn't going to get by with anything around here!"

After high school Tony joined the United States Army and served honorably for seven years in the infantry. He loved the military, claiming the routine and rigorous rules were a "cinch" after growing up in this household!

Tony today makes his home in Austin, Texas, preferring the warm climate to the Minnesota winters he grew up with. He is a fun-loving, easy-natured guy with an outgoing personality. And guess what he does for a living? He talks! In fact, he has received awards several years in a row from Toyota for being the top salesman in his market. 🌲

> Discipline your children, and they will give you rest;
> they will give delight to your heart.
>
> —Proverbs 29:17

34

Responding to God's Nudging

After the arrival of Tina and Tony, we were *sure* this was about all we could handle. After all, we had four children under five years of age, and each deserved our time and special attention.

One day John came home early from work to find me lying across the bed in tears. "I know this was *my* idea, but I need a break, or maybe I'm just scared. It's such a *BIG* responsibility."

What I needed first and foremost was a deeper prayer life and faith. I had not turned over the care of these children to God and was trying to shoulder it all myself. I did not yet understand that these were *his* children, and he wanted their health and happiness even more than I did. He would give me all the help I needed if I trusted and *asked*.

Next John and I realized we needed time for US. We started "dating" again, even if it meant nothing more than a walk around the lake (there are plenty here in Minnesota), a trip to the Dairy Queen or a dinner out ALONE. We also resolved to take a vacation together *alone* each year. Sometimes it meant nothing more than an overnight, but once the nursing and diaper days were controllable, we managed days and even a week ALONE. These yearly rendezvous were wonderful and just what we needed!

Best of all, it was through my fear, exhaustion and insecurity that I reached for God. My prayer was simple yet sincere: "Lord, please help me. I feel so inadequate. Please help me to be the best wife and mom I can be for John and my children."

Prayer time for me became a daily *must*, no matter what. In fact, I learned to pray *while* I worked and to offer work as a prayer to Jesus. It's amazing what you can do if you invite God to work *through* your inadequacies.

Two years after Tina and Tony's arrival, John and I attended a Marriage Encounter Weekend. We were confronted with a question on the last day of the retreat: "Do you think you have all the children *God* intends you to have?"

Until then, I am sorry to say, we had never thought about asking God to be part of our family planning decisions. We had pretty much decided that "four was plenty." But now the Holy Spirit was setting us on a course that opened our hearts, widened our horizons and changed our lives. We realized that God had something more in store, if we would just trust. And so we went home and immediately began planning for another child. Adoption is where we felt called.

Daniel, Our "Forever" Son

> Deliver me from those who work evil;
>   from the bloodthirsty save me.
> Even now they lie in wait for my life.
>
> —PSALM 59:2–3

Within months we were busy hanging wallpaper, painting bedrooms and repairing secondhand bunk beds and dressers in preparation for the arrival of Vo Dinh Thanh, whom we named Daniel Thanh. We knew that our son-to-be was six or seven years old, had lived his entire life in the polio wing of a Saigon hospital, walked with a limp and wore a leg brace. And according to the nurses who cared for him, Daniel was "a happy, self-sufficient little boy."

We sent him letters, cards, pictures, clothing and continual "updates," helping to prepare him to come to America and his new "forever" family. The snapshot we received in return showed a handsome lad standing tall under a tree. His arms were at his side, and his shorts exposed a slightly smaller leg with a metal brace fit snugly around it. Socks curled down around his shoes. Daniel's whimsical smile heightened our eagerness for his coming.

It seemed our prayers had been answered. We completed all the necessary paperwork for his immigration to the United States. Then came nine months of waiting.

Outside of Daniel's hospital room, the fall of Saigon to the North Vietnamese was imminent that spring of 1975. Several times his travel plans were canceled because of the waging war and turmoil. We hired a Vietnamese lawyer to go to court on our behalf. Daniel was our legally adopted son, even though he was stuck halfway around the world.

As the war came closer to where he was, we became ever more desperate. We would be notified that his visa was approved and he was on his way, only to receive a later call saying, "Sorry, he didn't make the flight." Our only goal was to get him out safely before the country collapsed to communism.

Daniel was finally put on a C5A Air Force jet, one of the last to leave South Vietnam, loaded with 132 orphaned infants and children. Eleven minutes after takeoff the jet crashed into a rice paddy, and so too did our hopes, dreams and plans for Daniel Thanh. Our son died as he lay strapped to the floor of that cargo plane, the seats having been removed to airlift out as many children as possible.

There are absolutely no words to describe our sorrow. In our minds and in our hearts, Daniel was our son.

"What happened?" we asked God. "We thought this was *your* idea?"

As John and I held each other that April morning and sobbed, he uttered what we both wondered, "How could this be part of God's plan? Maybe we weren't meant to have another child."

On two different occasions we were offered healthy infant Vietnamese babies. Each time we said no. We knew there were childless couples who would eagerly embrace one of these babies, but what about the older children with special needs? Who would be waiting for them? We were.

Even in our sorrow and uncertainty, we knew that the Lord's plans are not always ours, and we began to believe that he had greater things in store if we would but trust and wait. And so we did.

Charlie, a New "Brudder"

> In this you rejoice, even if now for a little while you have had to suffer various trials, so that the genuineness of your faith—being more precious than gold that, though perishable, is tested by fire—may be found to result in praise and glory and honor when Jesus Christ is revealed.
>
> —1 PETER 1:6–7

Four weeks to the day after Daniel's death, we received notice that there was a beautiful little five-and-a-half-year-old boy (six months older than Timmy) from an orphanage in Saigon who very much needed a home and family. He spoke no English. He had just arrived from Guam, where he had been recovering from scarlet fever and other minor medical problems. He was thought to be either full Cambodian or Vietnamese and American black.

This was the child to whom my parents objected so strongly because of their upbringing. As much as we wanted to maintain a close and loving relationship with my parents, especially for the sake of our children, we just *knew* that this little boy was to be our new son. We said an unhesitating "Yes!" and Charlie arrived two days later.

Our household was joyful for the first time in a month. Timmy was the most excited of all. He was going to have a new brother after all, and one his "very own size."

When the escort carried Charlie off the plane, he was sound asleep due to the heavy medication he was still under, yet he appeared normal and healthy in every way. As his little body was placed in our eager arms, his head flopped backwards to reveal a mouthful of brown teeth. "Oh, dear," I sighed to no one in particular, "I think a trip to the dentist will be our first order of business."

That evening, as John and I sat at the kitchen table trying to catch our breath and eat a late dinner, Timmy marched in the back door and through the kitchen, followed by seven or eight neighbor kids. He looked like the Pied Piper, chattering nonstop: "Wait till you see my new brudder. He's still sleeping, but he's really *neat*, even though his teeth are all rotten!"

It was "love at first sight" for Timmy and Charlie. They looked like salt and pepper as they went down the street together: Tim blond and fair, Charlie as dark-skinned as the nickname the orphanage had tagged him with, "Ebony." Charlie could understand NO English, yet they had a way of communicating and playing together that many biologically related siblings never experience. There was no doubt in our minds that this bonding was God's way of showing us, "This was *my* plan for you."

To this day the kids recall Charlie's eating his breakfast Cheerios with chopsticks. He was neat and proficient. The others had to try. The milk and cereal went in every direction but their mouths. They went back to their spoons. And Charlie was anxious to use what the others were using, so he soon had a spoon too.

For Charlie there were other adjustments. Not understanding our language was certainly one. A tutor worked with him through the summer months to prepare him to enter kindergarten with Tim in the fall. And yes, his need for dental repair was extensive.

We also had to help Charlie become familiar with the things we Americans take for granted: running water, flush toilets, light switches, refrigerators and ovens. It was not unusual those first few months to walk into a room and see all the lights on or all the burners on the stove turned on high! Worst of all was his fascination with *running* water.

One early morning I heard my next-door neighbor let out an ear-piercing scream. I looked out the window to see Charlie, hose in hand, sheepishly staring at the neighbor, whom he had just generously sprayed with the hose as she stood hanging her morning wash. I marched out the back door, shaking my finger, waving my arms and yelling,

"What did I tell you? No. No!" I landed a well-placed swat on his behind to punctuate my displeasure.

I apologized to my sopping wet neighbor, then turned back to Charlie, only to catch the trace of a smile across his dark round face. He was flashing Tim a look that said, "I must be here to stay, 'cuz she's treating me just like she treats you!" I'll never forget his unspoken message. Truly, discipline is love.

The most overwhelming obstacle to Charlie's adjustment came at night, when he suffered nightmares. Gently we would hold him, assuring him of our presence and his safety.

Also difficult was the sound of sirens, which would trigger an air raid-type reaction. He would grab the other children and throw them to the ground, covering them with his body. Or he would run toward the house and remain there the rest of the day, too frightened to believe that what he'd heard was not a bomb warning.

It took several years before Charlie could reveal some of the memories that haunted him. Gradually we learned of the hunger (stray cats were eaten for survival), the bombings and the dead bodies he had seen in his homeland. Prayer and time healed what we could not.

Charlie and Tim were into just about every kind of sport. Short though he was, Charlie had a solid muscular build and quick-as-lightning legs, which made him a natural at football and basketball.

Charlie is truly one of our "miracles." He grew into a gregarious, charming and affectionate young man. After one year of college he joined the United States Air Force, working his way through college at the same time.

Today Charlie lives in Minnesota and has a degree in electrical engineering. His "spare time" is taken up with teaching CCD at his parish church, being a Big Brother, helping me with a Web page for PROLIFE Across AMERICA and "inventing" new computer technology.

Everyone loves being with Charlie. He has a personality that is genuine, warm and outgoing. And when he gives you a hug, every rib in your "cage" knows you've been loved!

Little did we dream what that baby lift from Vietnam so very long ago would bring into our lives. What a privilege it is to call him our son!

Lessons from Theresa

> For you, O Lord, are my hope,
> my trust, O LORD, from my youth.
> Upon you I have leaned from my birth;
> it was you who took me from my mother's womb.
> —PSALM 71:5–6

It wasn't long after Charlie arrived that we both *knew* it was time to add another by adoption. We had two "home growns," two Asians and only one black. Quite frankly, we felt we should round out our color scheme!

Theresa spent her first two months of life as a preemie in an intensive care nursery in Rochester, Minnesota. Dr. Hymie Gordon, of the Mayo Clinic, a world-renowned geneticist, discovered that she was vulnerable to a serious congenital condition, which later in life could involve major surgery. Additional testing by Mayo physicians found her to be a borderline slow learner.

Theresa was two and a half and living in foster care when we first heard about her. She sounded like just the one who could fill our void. Within weeks she was in our home to stay.

Each adoption, much like each child added biologically, means adjustment. Theresa was a loner, content to remain in her own little world. She did not join in with the other kids, even though they coaxed and tried to include her. Chrissy, the "second mother," was especially creative at thinking of play activities to draw her out. Yet the children's laughter and loud play only caused Theresa to cover her ears and move away from them.

Theresa was content just to sit—by the hour if I let her—rocking and sucking four of her fingers. Her teeth were already protruding outward, and by the time her permanent teeth came in, she could not close her lips over them. Thankfully, with the aid of dental care, braces and a retainer, Theresa had a lovely smile by her teen years.

As expected, learning was a challenge for Theresa, and her built-in stubbornness only heightened the problem. We read to her and worked with her, teaching her numbers and reading skills. We also played music and sang songs, encouraging her to repeat the words. Here was something she *really* enjoyed! "If we could just put the ABCs and times tables to music, Theresa would be a genius," John and I would laughingly say!

Working with Theresa, as frustrating as it was at times, was truly a blessing. I was learning patience and perseverance while she was learning her numbers!

The other children also benefited. They showed compassion and helpfulness when they knew she couldn't keep up. But when they were sure she could, they insisted she try. "Come on, Theresa. You can do it!" the kids would say. I sincerely believe that half the reason Theresa did as well as she did is because she was continually challenged to do her best.

It was Theresa who taught us to take the world less seriously. She helped us appreciate the meaning of the word *progress*.

One of our most gratifying experiences was watching Theresa perform on stage. She delighted in the attention. Her biggest break came in high school when she had a small part in two class plays. Comedies though they were, I felt a lump in my throat and tears in my eyes with each performance. The entire family and several supportive friends came to offer Theresa a "Go get 'em!"

The second most memorable occasion for us was seeing Theresa attend her high school prom. She chose to go with a boy whom she met on the track team at school. He treated her like a princess. Neither of them drove, so John played chauffeur for the evening. We paraded her before Grandma, neighbors, big sisters and brothers. She swished in and out of the car in her newly purchased prom gown and coiffured hair, with her tuxedoed young man on her arm. It was as if she *owned* the evening.

With the help of special ed and lots of family coaching, Theresa eventually graduated from high school with a modified diploma. She worked a part-time job at a local McDonald's.

Theresa had a penchant for the outside world and sweet-talking fellows. We kept as close a watch on her as we could, yet at twenty-one she became involved with an older man who convinced her that she could do whatever she wanted and didn't have to listen to her parents anymore.

Believing she was at work, we knew nothing of their daily meetings. Theresa was infatuated. Eventually she left, against our pleadings, and went with the man. Only later did she learn of his addictive, abusive behavior and the *other* women, several of whom were now abandoned mothers with his children.

Within months Theresa called home, pregnant, abused and "on the streets." Sadder still, the incident repeated itself years later with another man, who left another baby in his wake. Today Theresa and her two children, Tyler and Tahlia Ann, live together with the help of county assistance.

This is not what we had hoped for Theresa's life, yet we continue to believe that God is in control even when things appear out of control. Her adoption brought many blessings to our lives. In her adult life we have learned anew that parents can't take care of *every* situation, but we can offer love. And that we will continue to do for Theresa and her children. 🌳

35

Learning to Trust

After Theresa's arrival we figured our "quiver was full." We had about all we could do to be good parents to the children we already had. Or so we thought. "Six is enough," I told my friends. But we were "running ahead of the train," forgetting to ask God what *his* plans might be.

In the meantime our three-bedroom rambler was crammed to the corners. The closets were bursting, boxes were stored under beds, and our kitchen was so small that folding chairs replaced a once-matching settee. The neighbors joked, "We're wondering if you're putting those kids in drawers at night. Where are you fitting them all?"

We began to pray for larger quarters. Two years later our prayers were answered. It was a big two-story house right down the street from St. Charles Borromeo Church and School, the school we both attended and so, too, our children.

The day we signed the papers and drove away, I said to John, "It almost scares me to have something so wonderful and so BIG!"

"What do you mean by that?" he responded.

"Well, there's a Scripture passage that says, 'To those given more, more will be required.' I sure hope this isn't some kind of a sign!"

Yep, you guessed it. By the time we moved in I was suffering from a good case of morning sickness. And was I *sick*—and not just physically.

It had been nine years since I had given birth (Timmy being our last "home-grown"), and I was apprehensive. No, that's not being honest. I was *miserable* at the prospect of starting all over with a baby again. If I sound selfish, it's only because I was.

You would think that after having six children already, one more would make little difference. But I was looking forward to being able to do *my* thing! After all, I reasoned, I'd done my bit for God and country. With Theresa in kindergarten, I had been looking forward to doing something other than diapers and dishes. I was hoping to join a crusade, start a cause or just sit home and study the gum under my kitchen table. Obviously God wasn't finished with me yet.

I still get butterflies every time I think about what we would have missed had we not bowed to God's plan. I truly believe there are no "accidents," only "surprises." He had a plan; I just wasn't open to it quite yet!

This experience helped make me more compassionate toward the pregnant woman who, perhaps without faith, a loving husband or supportive family, rushes in fear to an abortionist and spends the rest of her life with regret. We were still learning that God has his own plan. Our part is to trust in him.

> For everything there is a season, and a time for every
>   matter under heaven:
> a time to be born, and a time to die;
> a time to plant, and a time to pluck up what is
>   planted.
>   —ECCLESIASTES 3:1–2

Mary Elizabeth

As this little cherub burst forth from my womb, the nurses and midwife exclaimed, "Oh, my heavens, look at those dimples!"

Grandma Delmonico, who was present at the delivery, could hardly contain her joy! As the mother of three adopted children, she had never witnessed the birth of a baby before. She quickly dubbed Mary Elizabeth "Dimples Darling."

Mary Elizabeth easily became the darling of her older brothers and sisters as well. They paraded her around the neighborhood and created scenarios and plays with Mary Elizabeth as the featured guest or visiting "child princess."

But it wasn't just the kids who went "bananas" over this one. John looked as if he had dropped ten years. He walked with a lighter gait through the back door each evening, kissed me quickly on the cheek and then grinningly asked, "Where's my Mare-Mare?"

I was spending most of my time on my knees, not washing floors but apologizing to God for initially objecting to his plan. I was so utterly won over by the arrival of our Mary and so thoroughly convinced of the goodness and happiness she had brought into our lives, I had now set out to *convince* John that she needed a brother or sister as quickly as possible. Babies have an uncanny way of doing all sorts of outrageous things to our so-called "plans," not to mention our heartstrings!

Mary made us both feel young again, and the prospect of "starting over" appeared fresh and new. She was an exceptionally happy child, easy-natured and undemanding. Her charm was disarming, and often she had us won over before we knew we were "had"! Basic survival skills for the youngest of seven!

Mary was affectionately nicknamed the "Sponge" by her brothers and sisters. As she grew, she seemed to absorb all the happenings around her and delighted in being the household "know-it-all." Just ask Mary and she could tell you "who Mom is mad at now," "who is in trouble at school" or "who has a crush on whom!" Nothing got past her.

Mary Elizabeth is selfless, kind and considerate toward *everyone*. She was also our resident "slob," determined to spend as little time as possible doing chores or keeping her room clean. In her teen years I enjoyed several nice lunches on the money she was required to fork over in "fines" due to her sloppy room.

On the other hand, Mary loved cooking, even as a small child. In her early teens she would often come home, put down her books, whip up a batch of cookies or goodies and *then* tackle the evening's homework. The kids, of course, loved it! To this day Mary Elizabeth is the one who brings the bars, cookies, cakes and desserts to family gatherings.

In her teen and young adult years, while the older kids were busy with college or on the go and I was still occupied with babies, laundry and endless schedules, Mary would sense my fatigue or a special need and quietly help with dishes, dinner and, yes, once in a while, even housework!

After college Mary took a job in marketing, a natural for her creative mind and skill in sales. She married Tim, her Prince Charming, and they too settled in the Minneapolis area. Two years later Mary gave birth to their first child, a little Irish towhead they named Patrick Dean.

As for Mary Elizabeth, John and I will always think of her as God's "special surprise." What a precious way to prod us on to widen our circle!

Angela Marie

> Your wife will be like a fruitful vine
>> within your house;
> your children will be like olive shoots
>> around your table.
>
> —PSALM 128:3

Mary had her own way of convincing us to have another child. Every morning when the older children left for school, she would throw herself across the threshold and wail for their return. Mary Elizabeth needed a sister—and seven children were just not enough!

With prayer John and I both came to believe that God was asking us to be open to another. Frankly, the credit goes to the Blessed Mother and Saint Thérèse, the "Little Flower," who heard my prayerful novenas.

Angela arrived two and a half years after Mary Elizabeth, on the birthday of her Grandma Delmonico, who nicknamed her "Dimples Darling Number Two." Unlike Mary, Tim and Chrissy, who were blond and fair-skinned like John, Angie resembled my Italian side, with deep brown eyes and a crop of brown hair to match.

She was a precocious child, oozing with charm and a flirtatious manner that not only stole hearts but also won her way on many an occasion with her brothers and sisters and father. John had hemmed and hawed with his "We can't afford to keep doing this" refrain, but once she arrived he changed his tune to "Look at our Angel (his nickname for Angie). Didn't I have a great idea?" Men!

As a toddler Angela was *very* independent and into everything! I'd look forward to afternoon nap time, just for a reprieve. Later I would discover that she had crawled out of her crib and eventually fallen asleep on the stairway.

The kids' excitement over Mary Elizabeth only heightened with the arrival of Angie. Now they had TWO to dress up, cart around and entertain. Tina and Chrissy became the quasi–Hollywood producers, creating skits for Mary Elizabeth, Angie and the neighbor kids down the street.

Angie loved the theatrics of it all, and to this day she is the most expressive of the bunch. When she's telling a story or recalling an event, her eyes widen, her face lights up and her whole being is drawn into the scenario she is describing.

The year Mary Elizabeth conned us into letting her have a pet white rat (in her bedroom, no less!), Angie talked us into pet rabbits. She and her little sister Kari, both adolescents, promised they would look after them and keep the cage clean. How could I say no to outdoor pets?

Our only stipulation was that the animals be both males. Well, either our "males" defied Mother Nature or we were had! "Thumper" and "Fluffy" became mothers to six little babies. We quickly found homes for most of the rabbits, keeping only two *males* for ourselves!

To this day Angie is our "gullible one." She can't help trusting in the goodness of others. The kids occasionally enjoy telling her a tall tale, just to see the expression on her face as she falls for their ploy "hook, line and sinker."

Angie was the busy child—on the phone, making plans, squeezing in one more event in her already overextended day. She is a "big picture" person, which often meant leaving the day-to-day "details"—such as what time school starts, putting money in a checkbook or gas in the car or mapping a route—up to others, most especially Mary and Kari.

While some of the kids may occasionally seek distance, privacy or their own "space," Angie likes being in the thick of things. In fact, after college she moved back home, saying, "I love being home. It's kind of the center where everyone comes and goes, and I get to be one of the first to know what's going on!" She loves a good time and comes alive the more people and parties she can cram into her schedule.

But her real soft spot is children. Even during high school, with its on-the-go social life and part-time employment, Angie rarely turned down an opportunity to babysit. She enjoys reading and playing with little ones.

Angie married Adam, the love of her life, who fits like a glove with our colorful crew. He is easy-natured, deliberate, thoughtful and *frugal,* which is why her brothers and sisters occasionally tease her, "You married Dad!" They are now expecting their first child.

> He will love you, bless you, and multiply you;
> he will bless the fruit of your womb.
>
> —DEUTERONOMY 7:13

Life with Vincent

> Trust in the LORD with all your heart,
> and do not rely on your own insight.
> In all your ways acknowledge him,
> and he will make straight your paths.
>
> —PROVERBS 3:5–6

After the arrival of Angela, Tony, our effervescent eight-year-old, kept after us. "Why can't we adopt someone close to *my* age?" After all, he reasoned, Chrissy had Tina,

Timmy had Charlie, Mary had Angie, and all that was left for Tony was Theresa, and *"she's a girl!"*

"I want a brudder, like the other guys," Tony urged.

We asked for God's discernment and felt led to an area in Calcutta, India. Working with a new agency, we heard about a child who was described as "seven or eight in age." He seemed to fit both Tony's criteria and our prayers. A few months later Vincent was in our home.

Going to specialists became routine with Vincent, as we tried to fit the pieces of his puzzle together. The abnormal gait in his walk was not reparable with "tendon surgery," as we had been told, but was a result of cerebral palsy. His speech problem was due to a "soft" (not visible) cleft palate. In addition, he had hearing loss in both ears.

None of this was at all disarming to us. We set about getting speech therapy, private tutoring and hearing aids (thanks in part to fellow parishioners at St. Charles Borromeo and the Lions Club of St. Anthony, Minnesota).

More serious things began to develop, however. Within a year of his arrival his voice changed, and he grew a mustache. The dentists and physicians whom we consulted for his medical needs verified that, in spite of his small stature, his bone structure and teeth indicated that he was at least twelve or thirteen years old.

In addition, Vincent was nearly illiterate. We sought outside assistance and special education classes to help him catch up. Evenings, weekends and summers I spent home-schooling him along with Theresa. Vincent was not at all motivated to learn, however. He saw little use for memorizing times tables or practicing cursive.

After our six-month "honeymoon period" (enjoyed by most adoptive families), the young lad who had come into our house shy, helpful and *eager* to please had become the family troublemaker. He constantly picked fights and argued, and he sometimes took or intentionally broke the other kids' toys.

Charlie tried talking to him. "Look, I was older when I came too. But Mom and Dad *really* care about you. They won't let you get into trouble because they want you to have a good life. They helped me, and they want to help you too." It was to no avail.

At about this time we learned that Vincent did not grow up in an orphanage, as the director of the adoption agency had told us. He had lived on the streets, where he had learned how to charm and "con" to get what he needed. He had been in a Calcutta jail only three months prior to his arrival. No wonder we had problems.

We began a five-year emotional journey involving counseling, family therapy and psychiatric consultations. Many of the professionals we turned to for help were not equipped to handle a child with such a deep-seated history of abuse. There were two hospitalizations and three out-of-home placements to residential treatment centers ordered by the court. Vincent was under constant supervision, and yet his behavior worsened.

An elderly judge seemed to have an accurate picture of our situation. One morning when we were appearing before him in juvenile court, he took us into his chambers and advised, "I've seen cases like this before, and considering the vulnerability of your other children and the hostile, uncooperative character of this young man, my advice would be to nullify the adoption. With his background as a street kid, taken from a jail in India, he seems hardened beyond *anyone's* help."

Relying more on the advice of therapists, however,

we told the judge, "Your Honor, if there's a chance to help him, we can't give up on him now."

We tried again for two more years. During that time our lives were no longer simple or carefree. The normal worries of childhood accidents took a back seat to our struggle to reassure Vincent of our love and protection and to monitor his every move, fearing for the safety of our own children as well as those in our community.

Vincent became even more hostile and insistent that we "let him go." He could not comprehend or accept family life. As simple as it was to all of us, to him it was a threatening and unnatural way of life.

After continual incidents involving the law, the county court put Vincent, at sixteen, in supervised foster placement. He legally changed his name from Kuharski and made a complete break. We were left to love him from a distance and keep him in our prayers, which we do to this day. 🌳

36

Blessings and Humblings

When I look at your heavens, the work of your fingers,
the moon and the stars that you have established;
what are human beings that you are mindful of them,
mortals that you care for them?

—PSALM 8:3

Kari

"Dimples Darling Number Three" burst on the scene just eighteen months after Angela, and by now John was taking full credit! Thanks again to prayer, my budget-wary husband relaxed and was open to God's plan. Kari became Blessing Number Ten!

Kari had a few setbacks at birth, including yellow jaundice and clubbed feet requiring casts. In fact, both her tiny feet were wrapped in casts all the way to the knees the year we took our first family vacation. Kari was our "alarm clock": she awoke first each morning and "clubbed" one of her sleeping brothers or sisters as she crawled over them to get to Mom. "Ouch, ouch!" we would hear, and we would reach down to scoop her up into bed with us.

That trip to Colorado was the children's first experience of an indoor swimming pool. John will never forget the expression of shock on my face when we walked into the pool area and saw that the older kids had lifted Kari, cast and all, into the water for a dip. There she was in

Charlie's arms, floating over the water as the cast came unraveled before our eyes! We whisked her up and dried her off as quickly as we could, saving what was salvageable of the bandage wrappings until we could return home and get to the doctor.

Kari was even more colicky than her "tummy" brothers and sisters. The kids tagged her "Cranky Kari" her first year. She also had endless ear infections and for a time suffered a hearing loss, all of which helped explain her cranky disposition. We nursed her, humored her and loved her. The kids carted her around, finding endless ways to keep her attention and entertain her.

I tell this now because Kari, without a doubt, is one of the sweetest, kindest, most easy-natured individuals I know! Once she got over the "crabbies," she was a charm!

She is also very thoughtful. One example of her ingenuity and eagerness to please others comes from a Christmas when she was about seven years old. She worked for weeks to create just the right gifts for everyone in the family. There was a restrung yo-yo and marbles for her older brothers, a tissue holder (filled with my tissue) for a big sister, jewelry cases made from egg cartons and cotton balls for her other sisters, a slightly used toothbrush for Dominic and for Mom an empty tube of lipstick filled to the brim with Vaseline. Watching her present her cherished gifts to each member of the family brought tears to my eyes.

Kari, nicknamed "B.G." (Baby Girl) by her father, seemed to offer in humor and wit what Angie offered in imagination and creativity.

For the first dozen years of her life Kari seemed content to follow the whims and wishes of whatever Mary and Angie came up with. They were like the "Three

Musketeers," doing almost everything together. Kari and Angie, especially close in age, even loved dressing alike. In fact, one year they wrote on their Christmas wish list to Santa: "Please bring us the same clothes so we can be twins!" To this day the three "Little Girls" (as they are called by the older kids) enjoy a special camaraderie and friendship.

As Kari came to her teen years, her thirst for "doing something new" took us all by surprise. One summer she worked as a historic guide on Mackinac Island. "I think it would be cool to dress up in those turn-of-the-century bonnets and big hoop dresses and meet lots of tourists," she reasoned. She loved it.

Another year she and Angie saved their money and went to World Youth Day in Paris. Kari was the "banker" and interpreter; Angie, the social coordinator (remember, that is where she first met her future husband, Adam).

As a college student, Kari worked to pay most of her tuition expenses, yet she still squeezed in a trip during spring break to work with needy families in the Appalachia area. After that she headed to Rome for six months as part of a Catholic Studies Program with St. Thomas University. Her taste for travel and meeting new people broadened with each experience.

During her college years she met Drew, a patient young man who admired her "spunk" and adventuresome ways.

After graduating from college Kari signed up as a volunteer with NET ministries, a Catholic national evangelization outreach to teens, "challenging young Catholics to love Christ and embrace the life of the church." This required a one-year commitment—away from home, family and you-know-who.

"I just knew God was asking me to do this," Kari said.

"I couldn't make any other plans for my life until I do this first."

Drew patiently waited. A month after she returned, he asked our permission to marry Kari, saying, "This last year was the real test. I knew I didn't want to live my life without her!"

And so as we prepare for their upcoming wedding, we welcome another family member who will "fit right in."

Michael

> Before I formed you in the womb I knew you,
> and before you were born I consecrated you.
> —JEREMIAH 1:5

When Michael Joseph arrived on the "Ides of March," nearly two years after Kari, his big brothers erupted with cheers: "Yippee! We've had enough girls around here!"

Joining in the celebration, the Archambaults, our good friends and neighbors, hung an eight-foot banner across the front of our house. It stayed up for several weeks at the insistence of Dad and the boys.

Michael takes after his Grandpa Kuharski in looks, stature and sweetness. The Kuharskis are big people: John's father and grandfather were over six foot three. They had even bigger hearts.

From the earliest age Michael exuded a sweet, mild-mannered nature that to this day has little room for selfishness or self-centeredness. This was not a child who had to be reminded to share or to "think of the others." It came naturally with Michael, especially when his younger brothers Dominic and Joseph came along. If there was a disagreement or conflict, Michael was always the one who gave in, although he may have towered over the others.

One of the most outstanding memories the older kids have of Michael is his penchant as a toddler for wearing Angie's and Mary's patent-leather dance shoes around the house and even to church on Sundays. He also used their matching purses to carry his toy cars in.

"Don't let him wear those," Tim and Charlie (age sixteen) would beg. "He looks girlie!"

Not to worry. Michael was all boy and just enjoyed the noise the tap shoes made.

Michael, like his father, is a sports enthusiast. In his youth his passion was baseball. On early spring mornings I could look out my upstairs bedroom window and see Michael swinging the multiple bats over his head (as the big leaguers do) or pitching the ball with all his might at our garage door. The once white door still bears the polka dot mud splats and cracked boards as evidence of Michael's vigor. He soon took on soccer and basketball, and as he grew in size and shape, it was high school varsity football, golf and eventually college football.

As Michael grew, so too did his wit and charm. He's a kidder like his father and loves to tell a good story. You might think that being "number eleven" in this big family, he would be lucky to get a word in edgewise, especially with three chatty older sisters. But Michael can hold his own in social circles. He loves a party and especially enjoys getting together with his brothers and sisters to play cards, shoot "hoops" in the backyard or play a round of golf.

When Michael entered the University of St. Thomas, his sisters Kari and Angie were on the same campus in their junior and senior years. Each had his or her own set of friends and events, yet for many a weekend or special event they made plans together, attending games or parties or just "hanging out."

Of course, the girls served as "advisors" to Michael on which classes to take and which to avoid. And now he's looking forward to giving the same sibling advice when he is a senior and Joseph an incoming freshman.

At present Michael is majoring in business and accounting, like his father and older brother Tim. He helps pay tuition expenses by working at a local gas station and delivering pizzas on weekends. He's energetic and not afraid of hard work.

The future is wide open for this guy, and we can't wait to see where it leads. Our prayer for Michael, as it is with all of our children, is that faith and family be the center of his life.

I know he will bring to whatever he does the gentleness and goodness that have always been the core of our Michael.

Dominic

Some may think that with a family our size, and in light of the fact that at this point Vincent was experiencing serious emotional problems, adding another would be the last thing on our agenda.

When we applied for adoption again, it was only after much *discussion* and prayer. We felt certain we were in control of any problems we would face with the children we already had.

Eve, our caseworker, by now had become *more* than an adoption counselor. She was an advisor and trusted friend. She knew the ups and downs in our parenting quest, yet she was totally supportive. She often said, "If anyone can turn this situation with Vincent into good, it will be you two."

Dominic came to us as a foster child. His young mother, of Mexican-American descent, requested that he be placed with a "large Catholic minority family." We knew foster care was risky, because it could mean giving the child up, but how could we not say yes?

Dominic was ten days old when he arrived, nineteen months younger than Michael. We called him our "Spanish Star," as his head of jet-black hair and soulful dark eyes dwarfed the rest of his handsome head.

We eagerly prayed each evening for Dominic's birth mother and for God's will (hoping it matched our desire to adopt him). The older kids even asked their high school classmates to pray. When the news came that the birth mother saw adoption as his *and* her best opportunity for the future, we were overjoyed. In fact, we celebrated by going out to dinner, something this family of fourteen rarely did.

Without a doubt this little guy was one of the quietest babies we ever had. After a string of colicky "crabby" ones, it hardly seemed normal!

But as Dominic grew we realized that our "Spanish Star" was more like a meteor! He moved like a "streak of light" and was into *everything!* One year he single-handedly peeled the wallpaper off an entire bedroom wall and left his "free form" pen, pencil, crayon and marker drawings in several other rooms.

When "Dommie" was about four, we realized that he needed constant supervision, attention and encouragement. We had faced "high-energy" kids and behavioral issues, but we had never seen a child exhibit abusive, violent outbursts at such an early age. It was puzzling and perplexing to behold. We could have a backyard full of children, all playing well, and for no reason Dominic would take a bat, stick, tool or whatever and club one of the other children. No matter how hard we worked to modify his violent attacks, the pattern increased with age. Soon even neighbor kids his own age shied away from him.

As the behavior problems escalated, the phone calls from teachers increased. We took him to our trusted pediatrician, who initially diagnosed him with Attention Deficit Hyperactivity Disorder (ADHD). Later other tests added the diagnosis of Oppositional Defiant Disorder (ODD).

We began counseling but with little results. By sixth grade Dominic was labeled a "problem," which meant that he was losing friends and valuable class time. In the middle of the year he was asked to leave school.

Remorseful and determined to be different, he did fairly well in the second elementary school. But by eighth grade his out-of-control behavior—toward students and teachers alike—became intolerable, and he was expelled.

What was most frustrating to us as parents was that there was a beautiful side to this boy that seemed locked away. He could be kind, good-natured, helpful and fun to be around. At home he could be one of my best cooks, and he really loved serving the results. Yet the troubles and violent bullying increased.

In ninth grade Dominic reached a towering six feet. The medical diagnosis was changed to bipolar disorder. Within the first six weeks of school he was expelled. This time he was court-ordered to a treatment center for young boys because of repeated physical threats and abuse of teachers and fellow students.

Our hearts were heavy, but we were relieved. Perhaps this residential treatment, where we visited on weekends and he "earned" home visits, would be the turning point.

The "experts" assigned by the county recommended psychiatric therapy and weekly counseling for Dominic but also mandated that John and I submit to psychological evaluation. They required us to attend parenting classes and receive in-home family counseling. Here we had successfully parented twelve children, and in spite of our sad experience with Vincent, not one of our others had ever been in trouble. On the contrary, most were straight-A honor students with behaviors to match!

But one day in prayer it occurred to me that Christ himself was subjected to the worst humiliation and death, as innocent as he was. If it was good enough for Jesus, this little discomfort was nothing more than a "gift of humility" that I could offer up to God. And "offer it up" we did.

In spite of the years of therapy, counseling and special alternative schooling for Dominic, his abusive behavior toward me and others became life-threatening. One month before his eighteenth birthday, Dominic admitted to an experienced probation officer that he enjoyed "being a terrorist" and beating or threatening others. The officer looked Dominic in the eye and said, "You need to be on the streets, boy, where you will learn the hard way what life is all about. These people love you, but this is the end of the line. You've abused your privileges with them just one too many times."

Dominic left the following morning. Today he still struggles to control behavior that has only led to unhappiness and repeated incidents with the law. Our entire family continues to love him and pray for him daily. We cling to the knowledge that God loves him even more than we do. He knows Dominic's heart and the obstacles that hold him back from living righteously.

This is another difficult chapter in our family story. I tell it now in the hope that it will give support to others who have similar experiences. 🌲

37

Our Last Hurrah!

Our heart is glad in him,
    because we trust in his holy name.
Let your steadfast love, O LORD, be upon us,
    even as we hope in you.

                    —PSALM 33:21–22

Without a doubt one of the greatest challenges of our married lives came when John was found to have a tumor on his brain. Located on the pituitary gland, it rested over the optic nerves at the base of his forehead.

Within hours of being informed of the risks and necessary surgery, prayers and support from our entire parish community of St. Charles Borromeo poured in. We were too numb to pray.

We had all we could do to keep the rest of the family (ages two through nineteen) afloat while we dealt with the details of preparing for surgery and the eight-week convalescent period to follow.

If there was any humor to be found in the ordeal, it occurred the night before surgery as we knelt together to pray the rosary. Afterward each of us took a turn making the Sign of the Cross with holy water on John's forehead, where the tumor was located. It was funny to see his poor face dripping with holy water as each kid insisted on getting a turn to add one more blessing.

Surgery the following day was swift and successful, thanks to the skilled hands of a local neurosurgeon and a team of specialists, not to mention the prayers of people, many of whom we don't even know. The tumor was benign. Prayer works, and I'm sure the holy water didn't hurt either!

The neurosurgeon, internist and endocrinologists prepared us for other side effects, however, including infertility because of the damage done to John's hormonal system. Being over forty and having twelve kids already, this consequence did not worry us nearly as much as cancer, ongoing health problems (which we were also warned to expect) or death.

John bounced back from the surgery and seemed to relish his eight weeks' convalescing. He lolled around the house in bathrobe and slippers, feigning incapacitation each time he wanted something. At the end of the two-month period, he appeared to have more energy, more enthusiasm and more pep than I'd seen in years!

But all of a sudden I was feeling tired and sick to my stomach. I was wondering if this was the onset of menopause or just a letdown after our traumatic two months.

"Menopause, my foot!" my longtime OB/GYN said laughingly. "Congratulations, Kuharski. You're expecting!"

Joseph

Joseph was indeed God's "bonus," a gift to this seasoned mom and dad and a houseful of siblings. He seemed to sense from the moment of birth that he would be sharing life with a sometimes noisy and chaotic crew. He relished the daily activity of banging back doors and a never-ending stream of kid involvements—be they sports games, music recitals, school productions, neighborhood parades or outdoor play—not to mention those hair-raising trips to the emergency room or the principal's office. Joseph thrived on the busyness of it all!

The problem with a "tailender" is that he often sees himself as one of the "big kids." At the age of two "Little Joe," as the kids called him, was out in the backyard trying to dribble a basketball with the older boys and their friends. When Angie and Kari closed their bedroom door to talk and listen to music, Joseph wormed his way in, chattering nonstop and attempting to mime the tune coming over the radio! When Michael and Dominic set off on their paper routes, Joseph scrambled to keep up with them, talking all the while.

But the one Joseph "shadowed" most was Dad. He followed John around the house or yard, and if John was working with tools, Joseph was too.

Now, John has never claimed to be a handyman, and neither, it appears, is Joseph. His gifts of homemade "art" were items that only *he* seemed to comprehend. We would unwrap something, thank him graciously and then wait for him to tell us what it was. One Christmas gift arrived with nearly thirty tacks and nails and a half bottle of Elmer's Glue poured over for good measure. It held a place of honor in my bedroom for months before tenderly "graduating" to the basement. It was probably a wise parent who coined the phrase "It's the thought that counts!"

Ironically, this is the kid who years later handmade two beautiful pieces—a clock and small cabinet—in his high school woodworking class. Sometimes talent is dormant before it is appreciated!

Like most of his big brothers before him, Joseph loves sports. He played a bit of almost everything, but this year he announced that he was going to "concentrate" on football. In preparation he trains by running, weight lifting and "working out." He recently agreed to discard the weight bench that sat in the center of the (basement) bedroom he and Michael share, only to replace it with a Ping-Pong table the family gave him for his sixteenth birthday.

Joseph, now a junior in high school, is no longer the "chatterbox shadow." Like his father, he is shy and more introverted than some of our others. Also like John, he loves a good story and bubbles with a sense of humor that pours out to a wide grin when something fun is going on.

Joseph is thoughtful, reflective, considerate and kind, with a deep faith that he is not afraid to show. We don't know what the future holds for him, but we do know that he is one of our family's great bonuses from God! 🌳

> Sons are indeed a heritage from the LORD,
>   the fruit of the womb a reward.
> Like arrows in the hand of a warrior
>   are the sons of one's youth.
> Happy is the man who has
>   his quiver full of them.
>
> —PSALM 127:3–5

38

Open Letter to a Child

And now, my children, listen to me:
     happy are those who keep my ways.
                         —PROVERBS 8:32

Since my parenting days began, I've become an expert in three areas: persistence, perseverance and (you better believe) prayer. Having children requires a crash course in faith, hope and love. How *do* nonbelievers do it?

Christian parents in today's world must steel themselves against the leaky logic and phony phrases of an "enlightened" age that sells such notions as "Kids *need* choices in order to grow" and "Young people *must* make their own decisions and grow by *experiencing* the consequences."

Heaven help us!

John and I cling to the concept that children *need* guidance and guidelines. We have this old-fashioned idea that even in a chaotic world, with God's grace, we will not fail in our goal to love our children, discipline them and teach them manners, virtue and self-control. And in the process, with our eyes fixed in faith on that higher prize, we can't help but occasionally tell them, "Someday you'll thank us!"

Are we ever tempted to let things slide or give in "just this once"? I admit there have been times when I'd sooner give in to a testy teen than hold my ground. In fact, sometimes that ground has felt more like sand—actually, more like quicksand.

It is especially hard to resist the range of arguments that begin with "But all the other kids can." You know, "Bob's mom *always* lets him go swimming in this kind of weather." "*Everyone* in my entire class—but me—gets to go some place exciting for spring break." "All the other parents are letting their kids go; this may be my *only* chance!" (I hope so). "Kaye's mom lets *her* have the car and her charge cards anytime she wants!"

Hmmmm.

My kids truly believe they are the *only* ones who are not allowed to go, do or have…you fill in the blank.

"Just give me the names and phone numbers of *all* the other kids," I respond. They usually say, "Just forget it." I suspect "*all* the other kids" would narrow to a questionable one or two if I could get the names.

Then there's the ultimate zinger, "Don't you trust me?"

In a word, "No. We love you too much. Frankly, *you* we may trust. The world around you we do not."

I owe a lot to one particular son, whose name will remain anonymous. He spent his high school years creating ways to cause trouble, break home and school rules, irritate teachers and, in a word, "get busted by Mom." Later he recanted his behavior and let slip the real secret to our success: "I don't know why I did that stuff. I knew you'd ground me for it. In fact, some of my buddies thought I was lucky because my folks cared so much. One guy said he wished his folks would be strict like you and set curfews. He thought they didn't care because they said he was old enough to make his own decisions. I thought he was nuts, but I'm beginning to understand."

Music to a mom's ears!

When faced with a child who was struggling for freedom and independence, I have been tempted to post an "open letter" on my refrigerator:

Dear Child:

We aren't perfect parents. Sometimes we make mistakes, but please know that everything we do is out of love for you.

When you want attention, we're here for you. Sometimes it comes in the form of discipline. We call it "love."

When you want things your friends have, we sometimes ignore your wishes or make you wait. We hope you are learning about self-denial and self-control. When you do, you will have something far better. It's called strength of character.

When you want to get by with slipshod work at home or at school, we make you do it over and over until it is your best, because "best" is what we know you can be.

When it comes to telling you about sex, we say very little. We know you already hear more than enough. Instead we want you to know about modesty, chastity, self-control and the joy of a lifelong commitment. That's called *real* love!

When you want a newer bike, a car or room and board at a fancy college, we say, "Go for it, kid." You can work for it and earn the money yourself. Just imagine the work ethic you'll develop, not to mention the positive self-worth!

When you tell us that our family doesn't have what others have, we often bite our lips. Someday we hope you will remember that we offered something more: all the time you needed and all the love we knew how to give.

When you say you are too big or busy for family or visiting loved ones, we remind you of the corporal works of mercy and insist that you come along to share some of your exuberant youth. A thoughtful concern for others is the avenue to lasting happiness.

When you want to be left alone, to set your own course and make your own decisions, you can count on us to butt in. We'll offer advice, repeat old "lectures" and at times deny you the privileges that all the other kids have. We are your parents, and we want to share with you our experience and insight.

When you want to worship God *your* way, we'll help you get out of bed on Sundays to be with the family at church. We'll remind you of God's command to "keep holy the Lord's Day." Surely we can take time once a week to be together and publicly thank a heavenly Father who is so generous to us.

When you want us to ease up on some of our rules, we barely budge. We know that respect, obedience and submission to God's law to "honor your father and mother" will win for you a greater freedom. You will gain the moral integrity to know right from wrong and to *choose* the good.

When you think we should make exceptions because you have "special needs" or because you are adopted, we make few allowances. We see you as our *real* child and part of God's plan for our life. The "special need" foremost in our minds is our need for you and your need for us.

When you say you can't do it or want to be lazy and loaf, we'll tell you there's no room for pouting or failure. *Get out there!* We'll remind you that you are God's child and that he loves you and has a plan and a mission that only you can fulfill.

No, dear Child, we aren't perfect parents; we aren't even close. But someday we pray you will know that we love you with all our hearts and that we did the best we could.

Children, obey your parents in the Lord, for this is right. "Honor your father and mother"—this is the first commandment with a promise: "so that it may be well with you and you may live long on the earth."

—EPHESIANS 6:1–3

Notes

Chapter 3: What's in a Name?
1. As quoted in "Novena in Honor of St. Maximilian Kolbe," Day 3, distributed by St. Maximilian Kolbe Shrine, Marytown, Libertyville, Illinois.

Chapter 4: Too Many Kids?
1. Pope John Paul II, homily of January 1, 1980, no. 7.
2. "The World's Vanishing Children," Population Research Institute, 1190 Progress Dr., 2D, P.O. Box 1559, Front Royal, VA 22630. See https://pop.org/main.cfm?id=268&r1=1.00&r2=5.00&r3=0&r4=0&level=2&eid=829.

Chapter 6: The Gift of Love
1. Pope John Paul II, *The Gospel of Life*, "On the Value and Inviolability of Human Life," March 25, 1993, quoting his own encyclical letter *Centesimus Annus* of May 1, 1991.

Chapter 7: Unsung Heroines
1. "In Command on Shore and at Sea," *New York Times/Star Tribune*, December 16, 2001, A13.
2. Pope John Paul II, *The Gospel of Life*, no. 86, quoting his own homily for the beatification of Isidore Bakanja, Elisabetta Canori Mora and Gianna Beretta Molla, April 24, 1994. *L'Osservatore Romano*, April 25-26, 1994, 5.

Chapter 8: What's It Like in a BIG Family?

1. Pope John Paul II, Apostolic Exhortation *Familiaris Consortio*, "Letter to Families," November 22, 1981, no. 21, quoting *Lumen gentium*, no. 11.

Chapter 10: Taking Toddlers to Church

1. Saint Augustine wrote: "It is thy heart's desire that is thy prayer; and if thy desire continues uninterrupted, thy prayer continueth also.... There is another inward kind of prayer without ceasing, which is the desire of the heart. Whatever else you are doing, if you do but long for that Sabbath, you do not cease to pray. If you would never cease to pray, never cease to long after it. The continuance of thy longing is the continuance of thy prayer." From *Homilies on the Psalms*, Psalm 38, no. 13, taken from *The Early Church Fathers* CD-ROM (Salem, Ore.: Harmony, 2000).

Chapter 13: Boys and Their Toys

1. Wade F. Horn, *Father Facts*, 3rd edition (Gaithersburg, Md.: National Fatherhood Initiative, 1998).

2. David Poponoe, "American Family Decline, 1960–1990," *Journal of Marriage and Family*, no. 55 (August 1993).

Chapter 22: Parents Can Come in Handy

1. *Beginning Teenage Drivers*, pamphlet from the Insurance Institute for Highway Safety, 1005 N. Glebe Rd., Arlington, VA 22201, www.highwaysafety.org, December 13, 2004.

Chapter 24: Wedding Plans

1. *Familiaris Consortio,* no. 21, quoting *Lumen gentium,* no. 11.

2. John Paul II, "Letter to Families," February 2, 1994, no. 23.

3. Pope John Paul II, Apostolic Exhortation *Familiaris Consortio,* November 22, 1981, no. 86.

Chapter 25: How Many Priests Can We Fit at the Dinner Table?

1. Bishop Fulton J. Sheen's address to a retreat for priests in Gary, Indiana, 1972, available on audiotape, *Going on Retreat* (West Covina, Calif.: St. Joseph Communications).